CAN'T READ,
CAN'T
     WRITE,
CAN'T TAKL
   TOO GOOD
   EITHER

# CAN'T READ, CAN'T WRITE, CAN'T TAKL TOO GOOD EITHER

## How to Recognize and Overcome Dyslexia in Your Child

### LOUISE CLARKE

**WALKER AND COMPANY**
**NEW YORK**

Third Printing

First published in the United States of America in 1973 by the Walker Publishing Company, Inc.

Published simultaneously in Canada by Fitzhenry & Whiteside, Limited, Toronto.

ISBN: 0-8027-0392-5

Library of Congress Catalog Card Number: 72-80537

Printed in the United States of America

All text photographs by Tim Purtell.

Text design by Lena Fong Hor.

Proper names have occasionally been changed to protect the bearers' identities.

For Mike, who agreed to this invasion of his privacy
because he hoped it might help others.

# TABLE OF CONTENTS

# INTRODUCTION

This book is really three books in one. It is first of all a very personal document, a revelation of the struggles of a bright, determined child and his family in understanding and coping with his severe language disability. Secondly, it is a guide for parents directing them to danger signals which may foretell future language problems and taking them through the bewildering mazes of treatment methods. Finally, it is a "call to arms" alerting schools, parents, and concerned professionals to the problem of dyslexia and its massive impact on individuals and on the community as a whole.

To me, it is as a personal document that this book has its greatest force. Starting with the bewildering inability of an apparently alert, healthy child to imitate words when he was about two years old, Louise Clarke, traces her son's development through stages of restless rhythmic movements, poor motor coordination, and auditory perceptual confusion in the preschool years; difficulty with reading, spelling, writing, and even verbal communication in his elementary years; the tenacious quality of these problems and the emotional turmoil they subsequently evoked in his high school and college years; and finally his ability to acknowledge his defects and to compensate for them. It is an eighteen-year segment, from the age of two to twenty, in the life of a child with a severe language disability. As such, this book is an unusual contribution to the study of language disability and as such, it demands attention.

But much more is offered in this personal document. Although it was written as a recollection in the relative tranquility of success, it evokes with intensity the emotional turmoil of each day in the life of Mike and his family. Moreover, the Clarke family is not alone in the problems encountered here.

While his family for the most part learns to understand the special language of Mike's early years, they cannot understand his short attention span, his temper outbursts, his night terrors and the withdrawn fantasy. As with many such children, the professional dictum "he will outgrow it," gives only temporary reassurance and by the time the child reaches his school age parents know that spontaneous maturation is not sufficient to cope with the educational and emotional difficulties that arise. Early and accurate diagnosis is obviously needed. The endless rounds of testing and specialists—ophthalmologist, neurologist, psychologist, psychiatrist—all were completed, each with its own tension. Professionals in child care are more alert now than twenty years ago to the language disability problem but Mike's experiences are still needlessly repeated by children today and the child with a developmental language problem often is still called retarded; said to have a neurological disease, severe emotional block, eye muscle imbalance; or thought lazy, and inattentive.

But after diagnosis, what? Mike was fortunate in his educational experience in spite of being classed as retarded. To the child with a language disability, however the average classroom is not always therapeutic. Reversals, omissions, displacements appear in reading; spelling is at best phonetic; verbal instructions and lectures may be received as garbled static; and written communications are frequently idiosyncratic hieroglyphics. To all of this, the classroom teacher must respond with understanding, with immediate feedback correcting errors in a non-punitive way. The futility and indeed the damage created by forcing the child to repeat his work without immediate correction is vividly described in this book. Even optimal classroom experience is not enough. The child with a language disability frequently needs special educational help to attempt to compensate for the correct the ways in which he receives and executes stimuli. Simply to remove this child from the mainstream of education is not the answer. In most cases, the addition in each school of teachers trained in techniques of treating language disability, developmental or acquired, may be sufficient to keep the child with language disability from failure. This book describes the search for appropriate remedial help. For Mike, it was a long and tortured search.

In an interesting chapter transcribed from his own dictated comments, Mike describes the impact of his disability as he felt it, and some of the methods he finally acquired to compensate for it. His early years were characterized by the frustration and bewilderment of not being understood, not being able to communicate with teachers or peers, of being last in sports. He felt unloved and unwanted. He describes his difficulty with lectures, his repetition of errors when not corrected, his inability to reconstruct an entire image (figure-ground confusion). Teachers who recognized and nurtured his abilities, who accepted and compensated for his defects are remembered with warmth. He developed compensatory devices, such as the use of the typewriter, the reinforcement of auditory stimuli by writing them, the attempt to reconstruct an entire image by talking about it.

Mike finally emerged as a mature and successful adult. But as Mrs. Clarke says, "He had a family who refused to accept the verdict of the educational system and he was given a chance to get the kind of schooling that proved effective for him. In the long run, the greatest asset was his own indomitable personality."

In this book the days, the events, and the feelings become very real, while the perceptual and psychological defects we chart so impersonally and scientifically become monsters and mountains to be overcome and scaled.

But scientific objectivity must have its place. There is no reason now for any child to suffer as Mike did. Treatment techniques and diagnosis are now more advanced, more successful, and more available than when Mike was at school. The detection of a language disability in first grade at the latest is now possible. Singular success has been obtained by surving entire first grade populations to detect those children vulnerable to language disability, and treating them before they become educational failures and emotional and social problems. These children are not removed from their own classes, but they receive treatment given by a specially trained teacher, in daily sessions of fifteen to twenty minutes each. This is a promising, preventive method for the immediate future.

With all our ability at diagnosis, at treatment and at secondary prevention, the cause of developmental language disability still is elusive and efforts at primary prevention still escape us. Numerous theories have been advanced. None have stood the test of scientific inquiry. It may be that language disability is but a symptom, a final common path in which chemical, neurological, psychological, social, cul-

tural, educational and genetic forces converge. This path we
have yet to trod. It will be a fascinating journey.

Archie A. Silver, M.D.
Clinical Professor of
Psychiatry
New York University
Medical Center
July, 1972

# ACKNOWLEDGEMENTS

I wish to thank all those mentioned in this book, who not only gave so freely of their time to discuss the various aspects of dyslexia with me, but who also permitted me to watch the carrying-out of the several therapies, as they have been adapted to individual and group use. This includes the schools which graciously allowed me to observe a number of classroom procedures. I am equally indebted to many others who, out of personal or professional considerations, have asked that they not be identified.

The Johns Hopkins Press has graciously given permission to quote from its books, *Progress and Research in Dyslexia* in *The Disabled Reader*, by John Money and *Developmental Disability*, by Margaret B. Rawson. I also wish to thank Mrs. Rawson and Roger E. Saunders, past presidents of the Orton Society, for permission to quote from the Society's publications, as well as for their expressions of interest and encouragement. Special thanks must be given to J. Roswell Gallagher, M.D., and to Archie A. Silver, M.D., who made available reports of his work at Bellevue Hospital.

The Public Education Association and the Advisory Service of the Parents League of New York afforded much information and the response from the Departments of Education of the various States was of great value when I came to compile the appendix.

Mrs. Gordon W. Voelbel made available her excellent library, and Mrs. Harry W. Berkowitz contributed much of the information about the work being done in Atlanta. The young women volunteers who worked with Doctors Silver and Hagin did much to help me give a clear picture of this method, as they patiently pantomimed the precise procedures of the therapies they gave their pupils.

Mrs. Edna Gengerke, in the process of copying the manuscript became an expert in correcting my fanciful spelling. I especially want to thank my editor, Ghislaine Boulanger, whose enthusiastic involvement has been beyond the call of duty and whose suggestions have been invaluable.

An extra, special thanks go to Dr. Gallagher and Mrs. Rawson for the adaptation of their description of the dyslexia syndrome used in the title.

Finally, I should like to pay tribute to Miss Edith Norrie, 1889-1969, who first put us on the track that permitted this book to be written as a record of accomplishment, rather than dismaying failure.

CAN'T READ,
CAN'T
        WRITE,
CAN'T TAKL
    TOO GOOD
    EITHER

# CHAPTER

# 1

Most families have preserved a memory of some moment that was their "best of times." Our brief, perfect season was the summer during which our son, Mike, reached twenty-two months. Day after brilliant day, at our modest seaside resort, the oldest living vacationer announced that (*a*) the weather couldn't last and (*b*) there had never been another summer like it. Each morning the sun rose in cloudless blue skies, a breeze from Long Island Sound tempered the heat and kept away the bugs, while the occasional rain, that always seemed to fall at night, maintained a semblance of freshness. It was easy to believe that the glorious weather would go on forever, as endless as the succession of low waves lapping against the wide, safe beach.

Young Mike was very much a part of this perfection; he was the beach baby, the pet of the community. Mike was a beautiful little boy. The artists in our group thought so, and their impressions have remained—captured in oils and wash drawings—of pale blond curls, large brown eyes with long black lashes, and a sturdy body tanned a deep gold. He was everybody's friend and knew neither strangers nor fear.

The most enduring memory is of Mike's gregariousness. He made his daily round up and down the beach, stopping at each umbrella for his little chat. His visits could last from three minutes to ten; the conversations would be gay, serious, or reflective, each mood caught perfectly in the gestures of Mike's chubby hands. To stand back and watch the show when Mike approached a new arrival for his first talk was a status symbol that marked an old-timer.

The routine never changed. After the first minute or so, the newcomer, obviously flustered, would turn to me.

*Newcomer, embarrassed:* "I feel so ridiculous. Your little boy speaks so beautifully and so well, but for some reason I don't understand him. Is he speaking a foreign language?"

*Mother, gaily:* "Join the club. I can't understand him and neither can his father. None of us can. It *is* so cunning though, Mike honestly seems to think he is really talking to us, but he can't say a word. It's just jargon . . . our pediatrician tells us all children go through this stage."

*Newcomer, doubtful:* "But it *sounds* as if he's telling me something."

*Mother, still amused:* "I know, but honestly, he isn't—he can't. Actually, he's awfully slow at talking."

Mike's next routine was considered as diverting as his ritual peregrinations. The conversations would break off

2

abruptly and Mike would hurtle down the beach with a speed amazing in a small, fat toddler. He excelled at broken field running. "Quite a Lujack," as someone said, and certainly, eel or quarterback, he couldn't be caught.

Eventually he would tire of the chase and amble back for his third little game, which consisted of walking deeper and deeper into the water, until he took a long breath and stepped out over his head, always supremely confident that someone nearby was watching and would snatch him up into the air to hear his crow of delight at his own daring. And, of course, somebody always did. For us, as adults, it was all a splendid, entertaining game, sparkling through the inevitable monotony that a closely knit summer community produces.

Yet that summer—for all its brilliant perfection—contained the first signs, the first dark clues of problems that would haunt our family for years to come and almost destroy Mike. The very traits we found so endearing—innocent as the hot stillness of the day preceding a September hurricane— were to turn on Mike with results as unexpected and as devastating as the storm that put an end to our perfect summer.

Twenty years later, during an emotion-filled confrontation that lasted from midnight until well into the next day, Mike told me that our perfect summer had been a nightmare to him, for he thought then that the grown-ups were indulging in some incomprehensible and sadistic sport at his expense. He decided that he had been adopted and that was the explanation for our "preferential" treatment of his older sister.

The following winter, Mike, if left alone in his crib, indulged in a rhythmic rocking that bothered me rather a lot and his pediatrician not at all. Preoccupied by a flu scare that was keeping him busy round the clock the doctor was a trifle abrupt: "Probably going to be a Stokowski or a Gene

Krupa," he decreed, patting Mike on the head and leading me firmly out of the door.

Since he was being brought up on Gesell rather than Spock, I gave Mike some tests from *The First Five Years of Life* and he seemed to put the right number of pebbles in the right bottles and make marks which I, with the unprejudiced eye of a fond mother, interpreted as being those he was supposed to make.

Mike had all the very best books and toys. He liked being read to, but he never picked up a book and pretended to read as his older sister had done. In fact, he had such a short attention span that he might wander off before the story I was reading to him was finished. After watching Mike sitting looking at his build-it-yourself toys without making any effort to do much else, his father started building innumerable bridges and forts, that generally got knocked over by Mike before they were finished.

What Mike really enjoyed doing was pushing small cars around his room and going "chug chug chug chug."

Although he was not color-blind, he took no pleasure in colors or coloring. Except for a short transition period of finger painting (although I should point out that he was using nothing as innocuous as paint and only indulged in this messy sport after his nap), I cannot remember that he played with paints or crayons, unless I was urging him on á la Gesell.

In the eighteen months following that enchanted summer, he did learn to speak—after a fashion—and as he began to talk, we found his mispronunciations as charming as his jargon had been. He added letters in strange places, left off some syllables and transposed others, in no discernible pattern. The number was legion, the results unpredictable. Some were adopted by the family . . . "le-yo" (the buttercup

4

is le-yo); "listen to the frog (fog) bell"; "me last" (instead of first); we all suffered from the "heady-aches," and if the weather took a turn for the worse, Mike declared that it had "clouded down." He never said, "two or three"; to Mike it was always "three or two," and after he had discovered the name of our five o'clock drink, Peter Rabbit's siblings were immortalized as "Flopsy, Mopsy and Cocktail."

To understand Mike involved quite a lot of interpretation. The family was well-trained enough that communicating was not a problem most of the time, and since the two-year-old sandbox set communicates with three expressions: "Mine!" "No!" and (acted out) *wham*, he held his own, conversationally, with his peers.

By the age of three, despite his short attention span, Mike would sit quietly for half an hour or longer listening to "The Girls," as he called the first act of *Madama Butterfly. The Pirates of Penzance, H.M.S. Pinafore* and *Iolanthe* came next. Settled back in a big red chair, he was relaxed and happy, just listening. However, a curious thing happened that winter. I was playing carols, and Mike asked me to play "Deezi-Do." I had not the slightest idea what he was talking about, and as he could not hum it properly (for all his love of music, he could not carry a tune), the guessing game went on until, for the first time, I became truly impatient with his jargon. I told him that if he wanted to hear the song *that* much, he'd have to make the effort to say the name correctly.

Feeling I had handled the situation properly at last, I went on playing. But seconds later, a sobbing, scratching, screaming fury got between me and the keyboard, sweeping the music to the floor and crying for "Deezi-Do." I recognized a full-fledged Force Nine tantrum—totally uncalled for as far as I could see—so I deposited the young man in his room to

5

consider his temper and his manners. Nevertheless, the severity of the tantrum had shaken me so much that I phoned the pediatrician. "All normal boys have tantrums, Mrs. Clarke," said the pediatrician—who, I think, was beginning to wish I'd take my trade elsewhere—"if he didn't, you'd have something to worry about. Believe me, and remember I see hundreds of children a week."

Later that afternoon, with things back on an even keel, I happened to be playing *Gloria In Excelsis Deo*. I glanced down, and there was Mike beside me, looking up in sad disbelief, tears on his cheeks. He asked me in his irreproducible jargon why I was playing "Deezi-Do" now, when I had so inexplicably refused to play it for him a couple of hours before.

Naturally I soon forgot the tantrum, and "Deezi-Do" joined the Mike legend and the Clarke vocabulary.

Perhaps it would be helpful to have some idea of the sort of family in which Mike was growing up. My husband and I were typical New Yorkers in that we came from someplace else. We were born in the Middle West, and college educated, though without a shred of social or academic tradition. We had never heard of the Establishment, but then—for that matter—neither had anyone else in those days. We were not political creatures, in the sense that the young are now, but we had our causes—Loyalist Spain, the Newspaper Guild. Today we would probably be labeled middle-class liberals.

It would not have occurred to either of us that one could consult a psychiatrist about a baby. The closest we came to psychiatrists were the mysterious gentlemen with Viennese accents whom we saw in Broadway plays. They analyzed adults, whose thoughts would not bear examination from

6

their friends. Babies went to pediatricians. Besides, I was hardly a new mother. Mike had an older sister who had been brought up in the same environment, and Ann had talked clearly, enunciating her words in bell-like tones at the age of one. She had been a merry baby, very much like Mike himself. There was nothing outstanding about her, and though I know it is considered dangerous to say a child was "never a minute's worry", in her case it was true.

Mike, who spent such busy, active summers, seemed to close up in the winter. He had his tricycle at the proper age, but he never truly mastered it. It seemed to have a will of its own with Mike at the helm. It would head for other tricycles, trees, or buildings, and once in a heart-in-throat moment, it veered off the curb and had a near-miss with a passing car.

As the months passed and the sandbox play grew more verbal, Mike was inclined to sit alone in a corner, which inspired the other children to dream up the game of pouring sand down the neck of his snowsuit. At home, blocks made way for what are now called visually and kinetically stimulating toys. There were cubes that fitted into each other, cubes of contrasting colors, colors in contrasting shapes; there were clowns that interlocked into amusing acrobatic patterns—when we interlocked them—and all those Playskool toys that could be pounded into other toys. Mike liked to pound. Later, he discovered that a hobbyhorse fitted on a huge, stiff steel spring could be ridden across the floor, if he pushed hard enough. So push he did, with predictable damage to the furniture and considerable concern on our part for our long-suffering neighbors below.

Mike, unhappy with the sandbox set, spent a lot of time with me for a year or so. The old Third Avenue El fascinated him, and we rode it down to South Ferry and back, sometimes twice in a day. He then discovered the old double-decker buses on Fifth Avenue, and we used to stay on those until we'd managed to commandeer two front seats upstairs. It puzzled me that with all this traveling along two consistent routes, Mike never seemed sure which direction the bus or train was taking, or whether we were going up- or downtown. He learned to recognize some landmarks, but was always surprised to find them, and he could never remember on which side of the street they were to appear. I was also rather disappointed that he never tried to make out the letters on the billboards outside, or the ads above the seats in the bus, as many younger children did.

Each time the bus passed the tall building where Daddy worked, I pointed skyward to the twenty-eighth floor, and Daddy's office. Mike would kneel at the window and, follow my finger—or so I thought—until the day (after nearly a year of these excursions) when he became quite excited as a flock of birds flew out of the belfry of the church across from the skyscraper. It took me several minutes to interpret his jargon, but I finally grasped that Mike had no more followed my pointing than he had registered the right and left sides of the streets . . . he thought his father worked among the pigeons.

A seasonal pattern was emerging in Mike's behavior; one for which we had no key, and would not have known how to use if we had. It was enough for us that Mike—with all his quirks—was plump, healthy, and slept through the required number of hours in the winter, and that as long as he was entertained he did not seem to miss three-wheeled vehicles, balls, or the company of other children.

Summer was a different matter, and as he grew older Mike came into his own for a few months each year. With his hair cut as short as the barber could get it, he was no longer any-

8

body's pet or baby. He might not be able to manage a tricycle, but he had the freedom of a large safe beach where he could run for a mile if he felt inclined. Beach balls eluded him —he could neither throw nor catch—but there was the wet sand to mess with, and the water itself.

The big moment of Mike's young life came at three-and-a-half, when he learned to swim. The beach counselor—who had tried without success to get Mike to catch a beach ball, just once—took him off alone one day and sat with him at the water's edge, making a game of stroking the waves, first with one hand, then with the other. Soon, as they wriggled out into the shallows, Mike was putting his head in the water to follow the movements of his hands—left, right; left, right. The game went on, each time a bit farther out, until Mike found himself swimming, not—in the immemorial fashion of small fry—pushing himself along the bottom with his arms, but managing a genuine dog paddle.

The beach baby turned into a water rat. By five he could safely swim out of his depth, and by six he not only had a crawl stroke, but was so at home in the water that he literally did not seem to know if he was on it or under it.

This gave him a new game for the winters. I had an old green silk down puff, which, draped over a couple of card tables, gave him some illusion of being under the sea. Mike would balance on a low bench under the puff, and swim, left, right; left, right; for longer periods than he had given to any other inside recreation. The puff gave up the ghost long before he lost interest.

When he was four, Mike acquired one of those mysterious companions psychiatrists now find so portentous. Mike's companion from Never Never Land was real, a beat-up, cross-looking, little stuffed bear, whom he called Kitty

9

Pockner. Kitty lived an extremely adventuresome and dangerous life. He flew all over the world, and once his plane went down in the middle of the ocean and Kitty's very existence was despaired of. (In fact Mike had carelessly tossed Kitty into a hedge and would not admit that he had no idea where the bear was.) Kitty's mother and father—Mr. and Mrs. Pockner—lived in the rough, behind the sand trap on the tenth hole of the golf course.

One morning, we got a call from some friends in Connecticut who planned to be passing through our area and we asked them over for the afternoon. The Contners arrived as Mike was finishing lunch, and immediately he began to act most peculiarly and quite out of character. He was not a shy child, but neither was he inclined to show off, yet as the afternoon wore on he became more and more impossible. He dogged our guests' every step, and hauled out all his tricks. He had lately learned to stand on his head and he proceeded to do so at such length that our friends eyed him a trifle nervously. He plied them with food; he babbled; he was an utter nuisance. On top of it all, there was an air of tension about him, a fever of excitement that alarmed me. Finally, the guests departed.

Mike followed them out to their car, gazing raptly up at them as they slammed the doors and started off. More amazingly, he ran after the car down the driveway. He was calling after them, his voice tremulous with excitement: "Good-bye Mrs. Pockner, good-bye Mr. Pockner," until they were out of sight. Only then did Mike turn back to me, eyes shining with wonder, and belief in the impossible. "They came," he whispered, "Kitty's mommy and daddy came."

# CHAPTER

When we thought it over, this episode shook Mike's father and me to such an extent that we decided to take steps on our own without waiting to consult anyone. Mike's charming jargon was one thing; but to confuse the name of the *Contners* —which we had repeated at least a dozen times in the course of that afternoon—with his imaginary *Pockners*, was something else again. Pockner and Contner do not sound that much alike.

It also seemed to us that Mike was meshing his dream world with the real one more than he should be. Whether or not he missed being with other children, he must go to nursery school in September. We hoped he would find activities and companionship there, and that trying to communicate with boys his own age might correct his jargon.

The teacher who tested Mike for nursery school was not disturbed by his mispronuntiations. She found them "quaint." He must have put the right number of triangles in the right holes, since he was accepted, although the tests noted that in the light of his total performance, his verbal comprehension was "puzzling." One episode delighted the teacher. She threw him a ball and told him to throw it back to her. Mike stood stock still for several seconds, then turned himself around so that his back was to her and threw the ball over his head.

Again we asked our worried questions about his jargon and got the same old reassurances: "he'll outgrow it," the teacher echoed the pediatrician. They were the experts, so who were we—mere parents—to question their opinion?

At that time, all we wanted for Mike was companionship and fun. We considered that nursery school was for play, and I have not the slightest notion whether the play was "learning directed." I would probably have disapproved if I had found out that it was.

Mike seemed to have no trouble communicating with the other boys now that he saw the same children for longer periods. He continued his career as a miniature Marcel Marceau, and his gestures and inflections supplied his shades of meaning quite eloquently. Other children in the class lisped, mispronounced, hesitated, and—in varying degrees—used their bodies and hands to express themselves, so Mike did not seem too much out of line. The school ran through kindergarten, and the teacher recommended without reservation that he go on into the first grade of the school with which her classes were affiliated.

As a result, Mike was not subjected to the battery of tests

that first grade hopefuls faced even in those days. Since the school was—and is—one of the more prestigious ones in New York, there was a certain naiveté in our attitude. We did not search our souls worrying about whether Mike would make it but whether we wanted Mike to go to a *private* school in the first place. Because of our Midwestern background, we were as suspicious as peasants, and I had never even heard of such institutions until I was grown up. In the town where I spent my childhood, the public schools had been good enough for the local millionaire's children and it never occurred to me that people would pay for an education after having already put out good money in school taxes. Mike's father had seen his motherless sisters packed off to boarding school when they reached the age of twelve or so, and considered them vastly underprivileged. He himself had attended public schools in a large city. True, Ann was sent to a private school, not as they say for knowledge but to help her make friends in the big, unfriendly city to which we had moved. But not a boy.

However, we were not so set in our ways that we did not have a healthy old-fashioned respect for a good education; we belonged to the maybe-we-can't-leave-you-anything-else,-but-at-least-you'll-have-that school of thought. We visited the New York public schools and discussed them endlessly with our friends and each other. We came to the regretful conclusion that they were too crowded, with teachers more like jailers than teachers, uninspired methods, a poor level of achievement and a dismal atmosphere. We felt we had no right to experiment, to penalize our child by subjecting him to what might be a non-education.

Collegiate—the school where Mike was to go—was the closest thing to a first-rate public school that we could find. It was large, for an independent (as they prefer to be called) school, and it had a good representation of different creeds, professions and family backgrounds. Twenty percent of the boys were on scholarships, which meant that there were probably more students near the poverty level than in any suburban school system.

It seemed as near perfection as one could ask, and the year ahead promised to be as sunny and uncomplicated as the ones before it. Most of Mike's friends from kindergarten moved along with him. There were forty-two boys in first grade which was divided in two; each section was composed of one third of boys who knew each other to leaven two thirds who were strangers.

However, boys change between five and six years old. Part of the maturation process brings that very human distrust of those who do not conform to the fore. Any deviation from the accepted norm is quickly noted, and the casting of stones begins. Mike was suddenly confronted with a group of strangers who did not understand him, who did not intend to try, and who had splendid fun mocking his mispronunciations and jerky way of talking. Mike himself had matured to the point where he did not come home crying to mother, but suffered in silence. And he did suffer. This was his first experience of mindless cruelty.

His teacher chose not to interfere. She told us much later that she was betting on Mike's personality, which she herself found winning. With or without the personality, we would probably have backed her up.

Whether it was luck, or Mike himself, or the teacher's obvious acceptance of him—or whether small boys are not the complete monsters they are often made out to be—time did ease the situation. Mike made a convulsive effort and his speech improved. It was only when he was excited or tired that he would revert to his totally unintelligible mumblings.

14

His old friends *did* rally round and help interpret, "Mike means . . ." became a standard expression, and before too long, he was accepted. The teacher became his ace interpreter, and Mike was once more as well adjusted verbally in his class as he had been in preschool.

Then came reading, and the problems started up again.

I discovered Mike's progress in reading, or to put it correctly, his lack of progress, before his teacher did. He brought Dick and Jane home one afternoon and read to me, stumbling along slowly and with total inaccuracy. Spot, Dick, and Jane limped through their boring routines with much prodding on my part. Checking with the school, I was assured that this was normal, and that the little trio would soon go their way—as tediously—but faster.

Somehow I could not let the problem alone. I kept going back to it as one does to a patch of peeling sunburn, and one day when I put my hand over the picture I discovered that Mike could not read a single word. He was doing what any other clever, red-blooded illiterate would do; he had memorized the words to fit the picture. If he read *home* for *house*, or *dog* for *Spot* or *see* for *look*, he nonetheless passed, at school, with flying colors. According to the "look-say" method, he had "absorbed the meanings." We did not help him by sounding out the words or teach him his alphabet. The school had sent word to parents that it specifically frowned on such procedures. The brave new methodology those days, was the whole word.

Reading troubles were nothing however, as compared to the tribulations when Mike started to write. He clutched at his pencil as if it were a branch to which he was hanging for dear life. He wrote with his tongue as earnestly as with his fingers, twisting his mouth as he pushed the pencil labori-

15

ously across the page. Mike was left-handed and although most left-handed writing slants differently from the right-handed pattern, Mike's followed neither rhyme nor reason.

When he printed, the side of his A would start to angle up to the right, veer off due north about halfway up, and then add a final crook to the left before the apex. The down stroke would be similar, although never the same length. The cross bar also had a mind of its own, and was inclined to straggle. The teacher said he was holding his pencil wrongly and that we must not upset him; he soon would learn to hold it correctly, and all would be well.

Mike did not learn. He grabbed at his pencil more and more tensely and desperately as the year wore on. In second grade, he held it precisely as he had done in his first months of first grade. He remained incapable of copying out the simplest words. Mirror reading, or spelling, I could have understood; I might even have bought him a mirror. But this was not as simple as mirror reading—when Mike *looked* at "barn" he copied "rban." Later, when he was demonstrating his talents (he seemed to think he was pretty good), I said in exasperation, "Mike, your writing looks just like the way you talk!" Even when he took it more slowly, it made not the slightest difference. The end result looked like a messy version of Pick-Up-Sticks.

School continued to send home soothing reports. Mike was a bright boy. His attention span left much to be desired, but many children—particularly boys—had interludes during which they tended to wriggle and squirm and have under-the-desk fights with the boy across the aisle.

"My butterflies," the teacher called them. She solved it in the case of Mike and three or four others, by letting them perch on their desks when their fidgeting reached the point where it distracted the rest of the class. We were relieved to

16

hear that Mike had company as a squirmer. Possibly they were not as badly off as he was, but then it was all a matter of degree—teacher reminded us—and time would take care of all.


At home we had a more serious condition to worry us. The plump, placid baby who ate as much as we could shovel into his mouth, who slept like a top, whose tantrums were airily explained away by Gesell, was getting thinner and thinner. I suppose Mike's weight loss had been going on gradually all winter, so we had not noticed, until the shock, when his class was taken on a trip in late spring and commemorative pictures were taken with Mike conspicuously dead center.

He looked sick. His face was so thin that it looked like a narrow white strip between two enormous ears. We had never noticed before that Mike had larger than ordinary ears, now, looking at him surreptitiously we agreed that they were not abnormal, they only appeared so in stark contrast to his drawn face. His large brown eyes now seemed to have become enormous pools of unhappy darkness.

We rushed back to his old friend, the pediatrician. Dr. Grover gave him a more than usually thorough examination, and diagnosed the condition as "losing that baby fat."

Then Mike began having frightful nightmares. He would wake up screaming, completely disoriented and bathed in sweat. We would rush to pick him up, carrying him around the house, while he sobbed incomprehensibly about something that was "after him." During these nightly terrors he reverted to the jargon; he would start a phrase but break off and begin screaming again, before we had any idea what he was going to say.

When he had quieted down and we had put him back in his

bed, it would start all over again. Neither books we read nor the several doctors we consulted were of any help. We learned the hard way—and after many months—that Mike, although he responded to his name, nodded "yes" or "no" to our questions, was not awake at all. The moment we put him down the nightmares returned. We had to keep him active, walking with him and talking incessantly, for as much as an hour, until we were certain he was awake. Then we could put him down. He would smile up at us, and relax into deep, exhausted slumber.

If the doctors were of no help, neither was our old mentor, Gesell. Look up your old Gesell and Ilg—unless you read the gospel according to Saint Spock and do not own one—and you will see that Gesell points out that all boys have nightmares, that it is a part of the universal maturing process, and that these nightmares are frightening to parents, who should not become alarmed.

Mike became more and more pathetic; he began to dread going to bed. He wanted to sleep with me. Back we went to the pediatrician. Dr. Grover, in the meantime, had been boning up on child psychology. He took me into his office and lectured me on the dire results of letting Mike do any such thing. Did I want him to turn out a homosexual?

Of course not.

Did I want the nightmares to be prolonged for years and years because I had selfishly not faced this minor syndrome in an adult fashion, by allowing it to disappear after the correct span of time?

Of course not!

He fed me back a bit more of this new psychology, patted me on the shoulder, agreed that it was hard on me (what about Mike?), and repeated that I must be strong and bear

18

with it. Mike, that sturdy, well-adjusted child, clear-eyed, and puppy-fat-free, would be ready to take on the world any minute now.

Gulping down my anxiety I went home, vowing not to be selfish and to shut my ears and my mind to Mike's desperate if unspoken plea to us not to leave him alone.

The climax came very late one cold winter's night when I heard a stirring outside my door. There was Mike, huddled inadequately inside a ball of blankets, as near to human companionship as he dared get.

Did I take him by the hand and lead this small, shivering morsel back to his room, explaining that I was doing it for his own good? I did not. I responded as I would have done to any miserable young animal I had found on my doorstep. I picked up the chilled little body, huddled it next to me under the blankets, and held it closely until I could feel warmth steal through it and see that Mike had relaxed into deep sleep. The hell with it, I decided then and there, if Mike was going to be a homosexual he was going to be a homosexual, but I was damned if he was going to die of pneumonia in front of my bedroom door.

The results defy Dr. Grover's prognosis. Before daylight, Mike woke up and announced sleepily that he couldn't see how Daddy ever managed to sleep with me when I flopped around as he claimed I did. Then he trotted off to his own bed, never slept with me again, and never had another nightmare. He is not a homosexual.

I never did have the guts to tell the pediatrician why Mike stopped having nightmares.

Unfortunately, this had no effect on his difficulties at school. Mike did not read or write or learn any faster or better; nor did he regain any weight. His face was less miserable, his eyes less enormous now that he was sleeping better, but it was obvious that he was under great strain.

There was a new area of incompetence too. Mike's school was very big on athletics. All the men teachers directed at least one sport, and starting in second grade there was a great deal of talk about who made what team.

Mike did not make any.

When the top boys—chosen for their athletic prowess—were named captains, and the opposing teams chose their sides, Mike was always taken with great reluctance, if at all. It must be admitted that Mike was pure poison to any team. He could be counted on to strike out, to miss the simplest catch, and almost singlehandedly to lose any game of baseball. In the winter when the basketball tryouts began, he could not hold the ball, let alone throw it in the right direction.

Mr. Klein, the athletic director, was openly contemptuous, and the best Mike got from any of the male staff was amused tolerance. He wanted very much to make a team, and during vacations he and his father threw balls back and forth, or his father would throw them for him to bat. It was an endless exercise. There is a deep gully running along one side of our yard, half full of dried leaves, and buried in those leaves are the countless balls that Mike missed. It is too bad that baseballs are not suited to the composition of compost heaps.

Mike never did get the knack of it. He would miss catches by fractions of inches, but near-misses do not count in games. His batting was so erratic that his father—no mean athlete: he had won his letter at college—could not field them half the time . . . the half that Mike connected at all. Finally, when he had come closer to beaning his own son full in the face than he cared to remember, his father called a halt.

It was too bad that no one at school could have seen Mike

swim. At seven, he was racing with and beating the nine-year-olds. There is a picture of a rather smug Mike, holding a cup nearly as long as his arm, as high point scorer for the season.

There was a definite pattern in all this. The winter Mike was tense, white, thin, his nails bitten to the quick despite the foul-tasting medicine we put on to discourage the biting, and he was pretty much of a failure in school. The summer Mike, on the other hand, was not so much thin as wiry and lean. He was successful enough in the water to be rather cocky about it, and he was reasonably naughty.

Third grade started badly. By now he was supposed to be writing script, and the stories from his reader were taking on a semblance of meaning. There were also social studies and arithmetic, all of which depended on the primary skills: reading and writing. Yet Mike was precisely where he had been at the end of first grade. If he looked at a page long enough, he could give you the gist of it. Given the same words two pages later, in a different context, he was lost. Arithmetic was as great a disaster. Since the sum of 54 + 89 is not the same as that of 45 + 98, and since Mike never seemed sure which he was adding, he was no boy genius in this subject. This was the year when the teacher called his writing "hen tracks," and after I saw one of his papers I had to agree with her. With the best will in the world I could not guess what Mike was supposed to be writing about. There were letters jammed together in varying lengths into what I took to be words; those letters that could be deciphered looked more like a scrambled game of Scrabble than anything else. I sat down beside Mike and made a jolting discovery. *He knew what he had written.* Furthermore, with him to do the decoding, the answers were correct. I remember "Nloond"

21

particularly. It was in answer to a question on the third line down, over to the right of the page. "London," Mike said impatiently. There was another shock when, around to the left, I recognized "le-yo", our old friend from Mike's jargon days.

I did not have much time to brood over this strange paper and its inconsistencies, what they meant, and what we could do about it. (Should we get special glasses or a hearing aid? Mike might have a short attention span, play terrible baseball and not be interested in reading, but he was going to have to do some catching up soon.) Two days after my discovery, we got a call from school. Would both his father and I come over for a chat with Mike's teacher? This was so unusual in a non-parent-oriented school that we were apprehensive.

But nothing at all could have prepared us for the half hour we spent with Mike's teacher in the headmaster's office. Gently, but firmly, teacher and headmaster broke the news.

Regretfully, but irrevocably, they had come to the conclusion that Mike was retarded. They agreed that they were greatly responsible for not having noted it before, that they were guilty of unforgivable tardiness in only now arriving at their present diagnosis. The school remedial reading specialist had tested Mike, and her verdict was inescapable.

There was no place in Collegiate, they told us, for a boy with Mike's patent inability to learn. He would have to be taken out of Collegiate, and they would do their best to help us find a place for him in a school for "special" children.

We walked out of the headmaster's office, down the steps, out through the double door and up Broadway to our bus stop without saying a word. We were stunned. Mike retarded! It was an almost unbearable blow, knowing that his life was going to be drastically different from the life we had imagined for him.

Doctors and teachers, whom we had anxiously consulted about his speech, his reading, his writing, and his nightmares —which now in retrospect loomed much more frighteningly than they had when tucked away in the antiseptic pages of Gesell—had all been consoling. By our standards we had done our best, and had—until an hour ago—trusted the counsel and judgment of those teachers and advisors. All the way across town on the bus I could hear them in my mind: "It's natural at his age . . . he'll outgrow it . . . give him time . . . you're upsetting yourself needlessly. . . ." We had been patted and ushered out of all those offices as if we were subnormal ourselves.

We reviewed Mike's brief life as the bus carried us home. He was left-handed, but so were lots of very bright people. It was a plus in our favor that we had not forced him into right-handedness and brought on a stutter like his grandfather's. His coordination was jerky, except in the water, but we had no more planned for him to be the all-American athlete than we expected a Nobel prize winner. For every failing we had been given the best possible answers, from the best qualified sources, the soothing, slightly patronizing "Don't worry about it."

Anyone who tells you that being told your child is "different" does not alter your attitude toward him is self-deluding. Of course it does. I know that we looked at Mike with enquiring eyes when he came home that night. Surreptitiously we searched for the symptoms we had not seen before. We wondered about every move he made, from the way he picked up his spoon, to the way he undressed. What was he saying or trying to say? What did it mean in terms of his fu-

23

ture development? We listened and observed as if we were strangers seeing him for the first time.

I had read someplace that extraordinary pregnancies and premature or difficult births might result in brain injury. The only out-of-the-ordinary external influence might have been that the gynecologist had told me I might swim until the seventh month of my pregnancy; he did not mention diving, and as that was my usual method of entering the water, it might have contributed to *in utero* activity of which I was unaware.

Had young Peter's arrival on the scene when Mike was almost five upset him? According to Gesell we had done all the right things as far as Mike was concerned, giving him double attention for every minute we spent with Peter. In all honesty, Mike's peculiar patterns and difficulties had been established long before he was five.

I looked at Peter, now three, and wondered if he, too, was going to be a Mike. Peter had started talking clearly at a year old, but on the other hand, we had joked that he'd be working on his master's degree before he walked. Did his late walking pattern have any obscure, genetic meaning? And what about Mike's crawling as a baby, lurching from side to side unilaterally? The simplest gestures and events in their lives were now interpreted as spelling out grim futures for them both.

Michael and I have always suffered from blinding headaches since each of us was eight. As an adult there are periods when I surprise myself with the ease and proficiency with which I articulate, enunciating words clearly and properly for a day or so. Each period of proficiency is followed by migraines which frequently cannot be controlled by any medication.

As soon as both of them were tucked away in bed, my husband and I began the discussions that were to be as endless as

24

they were fruitless. Together, we examined all those episodes that had bothered us about Mike, magnified them, and filed them away to be considered again and again from different angles. Naturally, as the talk continued it did not remain on a high, calm, intellectual plane. We blamed each other and dredged up forgotten episodes between the two of us that might have contributed to Mike's troubles. We reviewed family histories. Was there any reason I did not know about, why my silly old great-aunt, Jennie, had never married? All I knew was that her engagement had been broken off at the last moment and she had lived out her life, a resented member of my grandfather's family. Then there was Tommy, my favorite cousin; witty, endearing, state junior tennis champion, but —let's face it—he never got beyond eighth grade.

Mike's father had an older sister who was not normal, supposedly from a birth injury. Was this really the cause, or was it something hereditary? Could it be premature aging? Mike's father was grey at twenty-four. Did that have any meaning? Eventually we went to bed, exhausted, emotionally and physically, unhappy about everything, and no further along in deciding what might or should be done about Mike than we had been in the beginning.

The next day brought the realization that this sort of thing would help no one, least of all Mike. We took another tack.

We examined our own family patterns and came up with assorted guilt feelings about some of our habits. Did the crux of the problem lie in our reading habits we wondered? Every night after dinner we were in the habit of each settling down with a book. Mike could quite simply be rebelling against books. We might not consult psychiatrists, but we knew our Freud. Maybe he felt threatened by the printed word.

Psychiatrists said that some children did not talk well because they were not talked to. Possibly we talked too much? We considered mealtimes suitable for settling the fate of the nation, the world, the arts, and any other area of ideas that needed our personal attention. There was scarcely an evening when *Webster's Unabridged Dictionary* was not hauled out to settle the nuance of some word. We considered all this entertaining, but suddenly we wondered if we were being self-indulgent? Was there just too much of a good thing? Was Mike overpowered by it all? We had tried to include him, but he was not interested.

We then turned to all the other palliatives.

Mike's eyes were tested and he was found to be slightly nearsighted. But there was no astigmatism, no pathology, nothing in his eyesight that could account for his failures. We even resorted to that old panacea and had his tonsils out: "Maybe all those old wives' tales *are* true and his tonsils are poisoning him," we speculated, "Maybe his speech is adenoidal. At any rate, it can't hurt." The tonsils were removed. Mike did gain a pound or two, but no other improvement followed.

We took Mike to a neurologist, and further possibilities were eliminated beyond all reasonable doubt. There was no brain damage, he said, no sign of birth defects, no alexia, no aphasia, and none of the other neurological problems we were now learning about.

So there was no physical reason for Mike's difficulties. Armed with this expensive and weighty knowledge, we became tearingly angry. Whatever was wrong—and certainly, we had to agree, something was *very* wrong—it had to be the fault of those who were educating him.

We stormed over to school and said so. We became quite stubborn. We pointed out that the school had had Mike for four years, during which time they had replied optimistically —in answer to our every question—that Mike was a very bright boy. If they now said they had been wrong, was it not possible, we queried, that their first assessment might be right and this new one wrong?

The headmaster agreed that he and the teacher had relied on the testing of the school's own remedial instructor. He was baffled by the neurological reports, and admitted that this might be more complicated than he had thought. He suggested that we have Mike's intelligence tested in greater depth and more subtly than the school was equipped to do. He advised us to consult the best psychologist at the most highly regarded testing center and it was agreed that all of us would abide by the results.

The big day arrived—for us—but for Mike, the tests that were to decide his fate were an anticlimax. By this time, he thought all the testing was routine extra schoolwork on Friday afternoons and Saturday mornings.

We sat outside the office, sweating it out. Mike was in there alone. The tests seemed to take forever, but the results took even longer. They reached us three days later.

Mike's ability to "verbalize" was poor. But we knew that. We read on. In every other capacity, in every form of testing that did not depend on verbal skills—such as comprehension, or the ability to reason—his scores were "above superior," whatever in the world that meant. His I.Q. was over 130; his aptitude for math was at seventh grade level. We were gloriously happy, gloriously reassured—but gloriously confused.

How these tests affected Mike's school, can be imagined. Neither the principal, nor Mike's teacher, nor the remedial reading instructor who had called him retarded in the first place, had a clue what should be done for or about Mike. However, they did agree that with such a score it would be criminal to send Mike to a "special" school for retarded children, no matter what his grades were.

The headmaster—an excellent man with many other pressing problems to cope with—suggested that we continue as before, and "hope Mike will outgrow whatever-it-is."

At this point we are going to break out of our narrative and step through the looking glass to the day—nine years later—when at long last, we found the answer to the enigma that was Mike.

# CHAPTER

# 3

It is obvious that there was something very much wrong with Mike's learning process. Down through the years, our search for an answer to this mystery seemed like a blind man groping his way through a maze. In our search, we brushed against dozens of clues that we did not recognize as clues until the malevolent genie was identified: not until Mike was seventeen years old.

This is no detective story. It has been written to give readers the advantage of beginning where Mike and his family ended that sometimes hopeless exploration; to make them familiar with all the clues we did not see, so that they—unlike us—will not be faced with the tragedies of lost time and ignorance. It is written for parents, doctors, educators, and even employers, who—like us—may be variously frightened, confused, or even angered by the unpredictable manifestations of this disfunction.

The condition is frightening and confusing. Left to wreak its full havoc, it will drastically change—if not destroy—the potentially useful lives of millions of children, as it already has altered the lives of countless adults. Our hope is to prevent this by presenting all our problems with Mike in detail, so that parents, knowing what to look for, may assume the role of detectives in the case of their own children, teachers can do the same with their pupils, and pediatricians with their patients.

The culprit is a perceptual malfunction which remains an enigma. It is not a disease, nor is it caused by neurological damage; it is a disorder designated as *developmental dyslexia,* or *specific language disability.* The word dyslexia itself is coined from the Greek. It simply means that a child displays poor ability to cope with language, and it should not be confused with *alexia,* which connotes loss of ability to speak or read because of overt damage. The Greek word sounds ominous, but the translation is so innocuous that there is a danger of the condition being underrated.

The term *developmental dyslexia* is favored internationally for two excellent reasons: firstly, the child is not handicapped by the disability until he is called upon to read and write, and secondly, it develops (becomes progressively worse)—if it remains untreated—as the child grows and the demands of our literate society become greater. Furthermore, the expression "developmental dyslexia" has the same meaning for scientists of all nations. In ordinary communication, doctors and educators can use the shorthand term "dyslexia," assuming the qualifying "developmental" is always understood.

30

Many scientists in the United States prefer *specific language disability*. This expression is possibly more meaningful because the term "dyslexia" may be confused with nonspecific dyslexia—or the inability to read and write—which can result from any number of causes. For example, a child may be intellectually dull, he may have minimal brain damage, or he may have been enrolled in substandard schools and never have been taught properly.

The two approved terms attempt to identify the condition manifesting itself in bright, healthy toddlers, entering schools, who are genuinely incapable of learning to read, spell or write by ordinary teaching processes. This, in spite of the fact that they are categorically defined as always having normal or superior intelligence, intact senses (hearing and sight), and no emotional disorders. The condition is congenital, not the result of undesirable socioeconomic factors.

Whether it was called developmental dyslexia or specific language disability, it was Mike's problem and he was in deep trouble.

The world of all such children is so bizarre to the normal person, that even those who have spent their lives working with dyslexia cannot conceive what it is like to be afflicted with it.

When the Mikes of this world look at that word "London" they actually see "Ldonno"; or "Dnonol" or possibly "Nodlno." If the letters would keep their places—however improper—it would not be so difficult, but they skip about and play tricks. In the early grades the child does not realize he is seeing the words differently while his teacher and classmates cannot imagine what he sees. To complete his misery and bafflement, the child quite simply cannot understand what

31

all the fuss is about.

It is true that some reversals of letters occur with many first graders, but before the end of the year the confusion is usually over. The dyslexic will see letters jumbled until he dies—unless he has had special training.

Parents and educators will find the multiplicity of terms used to attempt to describe the condition, as confusing as the disability itself. The condition also has been called *word blindness*, and the term is still favored in some European countries. The connotation of true blindness, however, is misleading. Another term that the reader may have come upon is *strepho-symbolia*, another Greek word, which means twisted symbols. This name comes from a primary symptom of dyslexia where symbols are twisted in speaking, writing, reading, and spelling, as well as in the sequence in which they are flashed by the senses to the brain. An early symptom is the inability to distinguish between *b* and *d*.

Other terms used occasionally are: *perceptual motor disorder, symbolic confusion, mixed dominance*, and *low skills in decoding*. They are all attempts to identify the villain that haunted Mike.

Precisely what causes developmental dyslexia is still being debated. But whether it is a matter of maturation lag, mixed dominance, or the delayed myelination of nerve fibers, the effect on the child is identical and the symptoms are the same.

J. Roswell Gallagher, M.D., at that time physician in charge of the Adolescent Unit of the Children's Medical Center in Boston, has proposed this accepted definition:

Specific language disability is one of the many causes of scholastic failure; it is a handicap to the pupil, even though failure may not result. Its basic cause—though

32

still unknown—would seem to be a disturbance in the neurological function, but it should be distinguished from neurological disorders which are less amenable to treatment (i.e., real sensory and intellectual deficiencies, emotional disturbances).

Dr. Gallagher later simplified his definition, to *Can't Read, Can't Spell* the title of a paper he wrote on the subject. When it was suggested that all phases of the disability would be covered if he added "Can't write or talk so good either," he amiably agreed that this indeed summed up the case.

Since the experts agree that all of these terms are no more than attempts to explain the disability, we shall use them interchangeably, resorting for the most part to "dyslexia," again reminding the reader that "developmental" is always understood.

Developmental dyslexia was first identified simultaneously but separately in 1896 and 1897 by two English doctors, W. Pringle Morgan and James Kerr, the latter a school physician. Another English doctor, James Hinshelwood, who began studying the syndrome at the same time, was more cautious in publishing his discoveries, but when his work did appear in 1917 his conclusions were both devastating and dramatic. He noted that dyslexic children were likely to be "harshly treated as imbeciles or incorrigibles and either neglected or punished for a defect for which they are in no wise responsible." In the opinion of most therapists this pertinent observation remains unheeded today.

Readers may still ask whether we are not upgrading dyslexia to the status of a major rather than a minor problem. Although it was identified seventy years ago, it has only been internationally recognized as a problem in the last forty or fifty years. Surely—they may argue—modern science and education are equipped to take care of the matter quickly and efficiently. Unfortunately, modern science is not all that well prepared, and the disability remains shrouded in mystery. Educators, therapists, psychiatrists and ophthalmologists do not know much more than they did then.

Meanwhile, the statistics compiled in 1971 by the Department of Health, Education and Welfare, and independent research conducted on a worldwide scale, grow more and more alarming.

It is estimated that, each fall, between 300,000 and 650,000 first graders are added to the ranks of the 4,000,000-7,000,000 dyslexics already enrolled in the school system. Add to this those who have left school, not to mention the families of all of the afflicted children and a problem that affects a staggering percentage of the population emerges. It has been suggested that twenty-three million is a low estimate of the number of people with some degree of developmental dyslexia in the United States today.

In March 1970, Howard E. Rome, M.D., Senior Consultant in Psychiatry at the Mayo Clinic, observed: "a failure, no matter what the cause, is tantamount to a psychosocial dislocation and a deformed social identity. The child reacts in the only ways he has within his power: he becomes 'stupid and lazy,' withdraws entirely into himself (such a nice boy; so quiet and well behaved: I can't believe he could have done it), or acts out his frustrations in hostile, destructive anger."

In Dr. Rome's words:

"There is a body of cumulative evidence which holds that a significant number of juvenile delinquents have reading problems . . . those whom society extrudes

34

have need to prove themselves, and in this effort they act out their problem by aggressive, predatory behavior. This is in accord with the frustration-aggression thesis, for these persons, untreated, are social rejects. They are the pariahs of Western culture, and this is their way of both proving themselves and striking back."

The president of the World Federation of Neurologists, Dr. Macdonald Critchley, also states categorically: "There is a correlation between dyslexia, adult delinquency and adult criminality. Politicians and government executives might be interested in research and training that would cut our dropouts and save the state millions of dollars by taking care of the predictable criminal population."

Dr. Critchley is an Englishman. In March 1970, the British House of Commons included dyslexic children in its bill to provide "special provision for their education in any school maintained or assisted by the local education authority." The Honorable Member who introduced the clause stated the case succinctly:

"The effect on a child who is unable to read, despite having an average intelligence, is predictable . . . social and emotional effects can be quite catastrophic. Educational progress is entirely blocked, and the scorn and ridicule of classmates can be a terrible burden, especially to a sensitive child. Once the spiral of fear, reaction, bad behavior, and truancy begins, there is no knowing where it will end. The whole of a child's life can be transformed by a so-called minor disability into one of failure and misery."

This all proves, if further proof is needed, that even today a child with this "minor disability" is too often condemned as retarded, abnormal, or brain-damaged—as Mike was—or incapacitated by emotional problems such as schizophrenia. It cannot be emphasized too often: the child with developmental dyslexia is not only intelligent but physically and emotionally normal, at least at the start.

"Let us stay away from this 'brain damage' stuff," wrote Dr. Lloyd J. Thompson, clinical professor emeritus of psychiatry at the University of North Carolina. He feels that the dyslexic child is often abnormal in another unexpected way, precisely because the dyslexic's intelligence may be well above the norm. Dyslexia could almost be called the affliction of geniuses, because so many eminent persons have been dyslexic. Dr. Thompson has collected a distinguished line-up: Thomas A. Edison; Albert Einstein, who always had difficulty with arithmetic and whose childhood frustrations led to tremendous temper tantrums; physicist Nils Bohr; the noted brain surgeon, Dr. Harvey Cushing; General Patton; Rodin; Woodrow Wilson; William James; Abbott Lawrence Lowell, president of Harvard, who wrote at the age of ten that "the name of the stemer was the Chiner, she was a propella and it blew prutty hard." His sister, the poetess Amy Lowell, could not spell, nor could Brooks Adams. The German bacteriologist Paul Ehrlich, Nobel Prize winner in 1908 for his discovery of a cure for syphilis, had such illegible handwriting that he had someone who could write neatly copy out his doctoral thesis. Some say Winston Churchill and Leonardo da Vinci should be added to the list.

Unfortunately, at the other end of the scale are the dropouts and misfits, who—less lucky in their environment, drives, and opportunities—fill our jails and other correctional institutions. Between these extremes are the thousands whose lives have been circumscribed by their lack of skills and consequently miserable incomes.

In the depth of his heart, the dyslexic knows that he is as intelligent as everyone else, but how can he prove it? It is the world against him and—eventually—he against the world. Dyslexia is not a disorder caused by slum living, though it knows no discrimination: the incidence appears to be the same among blacks as whites. The no-doubt well-meaning campaign of some blacks to introduce ghetto English in slum schools—in the belief that this will make reading and writing easier—is no solution, for the dyslexic child will also be dyslexic in ghetto English. There are children dyslexic in all languages, whether it be Hebrew, written from right to left, or Chinese, written from top to bottom. Naturally, any slum child, if he attends a school with an inferior educational program and disinterested teachers, will be further handicapped in that his disorder will not be discovered and consequently no steps will be taken to correct it.

The odds against all dyslexics increase as they grow older. If the disability is discovered, and remedies are administered in the first and second grades, the chances for complete success are eighty-two percent. If the schools wait until third grade—when by tradition corrective work begins—there is a forty-six percent chance of success. The percentage drops to forty-two percent if help is postponed to fourth grade—and by seventh grade the possibility for cure drops to ten percent or even five percent.

Although there is little to be done before reading begins, parents can and should get an early start by noting any untoward symptom in a child, and insisting that school systems pay more attention to that important first grade.

It is obvious that no child can bloom in the repressive, punitive atmosphere which is the lot of the dyslexic in the ordinary classroom. It is impossible to imagine what it will do to a child who is already disadvantaged, and who has felt other forms of discrimination. It is yet a further form of being put down, on top of the many other humiliations and social injustices the child may have had to suffer.

Dyslexia knows no class distinctions, but unfortunately, too many educators—whether in ghetto schools or expensive private ones—do not know dyslexia.


That is where we left Mike, in the third grade in a private school. We were totally puzzled as to the nature of his problem, and incapable of doing anything about it. The school had a remedial reading teacher, but this was not a question of correcting Mike's reading and writing—the kind of problem she was accustomed to and had been taught to handle—it was an entirely new problem, beyond her education or abilities. She solved it for herself by never seeing Mike again.

# CHAPTER

# 4

It was at this point that luck entered the picture; the luck that was to carry Mike through many rough years.

It would have been easy for Mike's third grade teacher to have been as disgruntled as the remedial reading teacher and to have taken it out on Mike. She could simply have accepted him back and sat him down, forgotten and forlorn, in the last row of the class, letting time run its course until the system passed him on to the next grade and solved the problem—at least, for her.

Instead, Miss Lever had been born with a great gift, the ability to question her own reasoning. Mike was a paradox—a puzzle—and she set out to find some sort of answer. Her first move was revolutionary, even brave for a very young woman with her career before her. It must be considered in the light of the times, for twenty years later it does not seem so earth-shaking. Miss Lever had been taught in teacher's college to use only the look-say method, which she herself believed in. Yet she figured out for herself that, while undoubtedly the whole word method was the very best possible for most people, for some incomprehensible reason it was not working with Mike. She asked the headmaster if she might experiment with Mike, to see whether she could find a clue to his failures. Out of the window went Dick and Jane.

Miss Lever's heretical thinking went this way: "Maybe his eyes are perfect, but we aren't getting to him through them. Let's try his ears." She dug up a system of old-fashioned phonetics and she sounded out his lessons over and over and over, with Mike repeating them after her. She sent home hand-made lists for us to recite with him. Sometimes he would put his hands over his ears and run away when we tried to help, and I know now that we were overdoing the exercise, but we were desperate for any way to help.

Then Miss Lever taught him the alphabet in the old-fashioned way, letter by letter, sounding each letter out and printing it. Finally, she tried to get Mike to put letters down on paper in his crazy tortured script. By the end of the year Mike knew the difference between *p* and *b*, even if he sometimes mixed up *b* and *d*. He knew the short *a* sound from the short *o* sound. He pronounced words more clearly, but his mastery was erratic, and his spelling was not much better.

The exercise certainly reinforced that learning enigma we had noticed before, the ability to comprehend what he could not spell. Now he would try to break the words into syllables, and could retain words for a day or two before he lost them

40

again.

For our part, we hunted through all the books we could find, none of which gave us any clues about the way to handle Mike's problem. Why could Mike grasp the sense of a printed page, and yet not be able to write a complete, legible, properly spelled sentence? Why would he pronounce a word properly one day and not be able to do so the next? At that time, the books and magazine articles about problem children thought they had found a reason: mother-dominance, because fathers were too busy at their jobs to be around the house. I meekly forgot that on the farm where I had spent so much time—and which was purportedly the essence of the old father-dominated America—father was out milking cows before the kids got up, and was so tired and cross at night that he had barely enough strength to give them the occasional licking they deserved. The mother had always been the home figure in rural America because she was the one who was always in the home.

At any rate, I went through a spell of conscientiously trying not to be around Mike or interfering in whatever he was doing. His father—whose job depended on his working weekends—nonetheless made Herculean attempts to get home and have a proper Sunday dinner with the family, while most of his associates ate that dinner right at their desks. Week after week, just as he was about to hop in a cab and properly dominate the family Sunday dinner, an important decision would hold him in the doorway of his office, while dinner kept warm in the oven. He would arrive, harried and tired, to find food that was either cold, or dried up. After one disastrous evening, Mike, hungry, bored with waiting, and near tears, asked, "Do we *have* to wait for Daddy?"

Once again we decided to let common sense prevail. Our attempts to set up the father-figure came to an end. Mean-

41

while, Mike was reading at the bottom of third-grade level, and the school sent word that it would keep him for another year, passing him on to fourth grade. This, at least, was hopeful.

We thought it another bit of luck when Mike was put in Mrs. Jackson's section. Mrs. Jackson was the mother of Mike's best friend at school, and Jim was at our house a great deal. Miss Lever's extracurricular help in reading ended when Mike entered fourth grade, but to make up for it, Mrs. Jackson—who was a whiz at math—decided to give him coaching in arithmetic.

Mike himself had progressed to the point where a 2 that he wrote looked like a 2 and he liked the security of 2 plus 2 equalling 4—it was something to hang onto in a world where "two", "to" and "too" meant different things—but getting the rest of those ten symbols—our numerals—to behave themselves, was a different matter. Mrs. Jackson noted that Mike could think through a fairly sophisticated fun problem and tell her the answer. But fourth grade arithmetic eluded him when it came to putting down the proper sums. She would make him do his problems over and over and over, and each time he would make the same senseless, careless (or so they seemed to her) mistakes. For example, he could do the complicated steps of a long problem correctly but then he would write down an obviously incorrect solution. Considering his aptitudes it seemed so odd to make the same mistake each time, that she began to wonder if he was doing it on purpose, to get more attention. If not, did Mike have some unknown mental block?

At this time no one could have called him a happy boy. He loved music and wanted to take piano lessons, but he could neither learn to read music nor, with his clumsy right hand, pick out tunes on the piano. His left-handedness was no help, and the necessity of shifting from left to right hand while he was playing confused him.

As far as athletics went he was still as inept as he had been. Recreation period became Mike's torture hour of the day. Only once did he say anything at home, however, when close to tears, he admitted that Mr. Klein had made fun of him in front of the whole school that day and complimented a team captain for avoiding choosing him.

Even the summers added to his frustrations now. He had his swimming and diving but he took those for granted. By now, his friends were going off on bikes, exploring; and Mike could not ride a two-wheeler any more reliably than he had a tricycle. It was his father, not I, who forbade him to ride on the road until he was capable of turning away from a car instead of directly into it. There was a parking lot below our house, and here, when it was deserted on Sundays and late afternoons, Mike would practice and practice with the grim determination of a boy who is going to master the bike, or break a leg or an arm, trying.

Dimly, we perceived that bike-riding might be a part of his lack of ability to catch a ball, but we did not connect it with his learning difficulties at all. Alone on the lot Mike could ride a bike perfectly, with complete control. What he could not master was turning left when he wanted to turn left, and not going right when it could be a matter of life and death that he turn left.

We had his eyes retested, with the same result: no pathology, nothing but the same old mild near-sightedness that had been easily corrected with glasses. There was nothing there to explain his inability to distinguish right from left.

During the last week of January, Mrs. Jackson called me

and asked if I could have lunch with her the following Saturday. Knowing how much she cherished her time with her family, away from the problems of school, I was certain that something new had happened with Mike. Whatever it was, she did not feel it was correct to talk about it on school time.

Saturday was a long time coming, and I was ready for anything in the way of bad news by the time we met. After a minimum of social chatting, Mrs. Jackson told me why she had wanted to see me. In her opinion, Mike should be taken out of Collegiate at the end of the year and put into a different type of school. Oh, God, I thought aloud, not a school for the retarded? No, she assured me.

As a professional, she reviewed the New York independent schools, which had a wide enough range to suit everyone's needs. Parents willing to take the time, could find some system of teaching to satisfy any set of pet philosophies, religion, politics, concepts of personal freedom, or anything else. There were schools so free that the children might spend a morning sitting on the floor playing slapjack, deciding—as an exercise of group development—whether they would go on to reading, math, or art, or keep on playing slapjack, as they often did.

This may be the extreme of permissiveness, but the more moderate shades were numerous, continuing around the spectrum to schools that gloried in their old-fashioned insistence on a classical curriculum and a rigid adherence to academic disciplines.

Boarding-school-oriented establishments for boys were the most strict. Their reputations were based on the number of boys that got into the proper Eastern schools. They stopped at the eighth grade. A great plus in our eyes for Collegiate had been that Mike could finish high school there, staying at home where we thought he belonged. Going away to school at thirteen was another thing we disapproved of in our Middle-Western way.

Now Mrs. Jackson was trying to tell us that Collegiate, picked for that reason and for its good academic reputation within the framework that came closest to the public schools, was not the place for Mike even if it did not reject *him* before he reached high school, which was a strong possibility.

Fifth grade was the cutting-off point at Collegiate; from then on there were all men-teachers, and the emphasis on intramural and inter-school sports was even more important. By the fifth grade, a boy was expected to decide for himself how hard he would study. If he did not come up to academic standards he risked being dropped (as it was phrased), "if the situation does not seem to be to the school's and the boy's mutual advantage." The schools that took boys through high school had their college admissions record to think about.

While Mrs. Jackson was talking, I was engaged in my own assessments. Her suggestion was not as much of a surprise as she thought it would be. Mike's father and I had discussed the possibility of something like this, although it was still a shock for her to suggest it. The school had virtually been forced to keep Mike, and no one likes that. Except for Miss Lever and Mrs. Jackson working on their own, Mike had been given no remedial help, and it did not promise a "mutually productive relationship" for the future.

Another small detail had also been bothering us. Motherly Mrs. Jackson had no more control over the boys than they had experienced in nursery school, where pandemonium was a part of the learning process. Outer garments were heaped in the corners of her classroom and some boy or other was always wandering around, rummaging for pencils or books that should have been in his desk, his excursion engaging the undivided attention of the rest of the class. There was much whispering and inappropriate giggling over nonclassroom matters during recitations, too.

Other parents had noticed the situation and questioned the procedure. They were assured that such things went on only when parents were visiting; Mrs. Jackson did not want to discipline the class in front of parents. Nevertheless it did not seem probable that the confusion had been created solely for our benefit.

We had also heard some grumblings from other parents about the lack of control of boys in the higher grades, of how they could manage to disrupt study hall and break up classes by taking over, and spending the hour talking about what interested them—such as the scores of the weekend football games. So we had begun to wonder whether Mike, with all his learning problems, should indeed remain at Collegiate. Others without his problems could learn, but could he? If Collegiate might decide that it did not want Mike, there was certainly another side to the coin.

We also worried about what Mike might have to face the next year. The fifth grade teacher—Mrs. Jackson told me—had taken one of those inexplicable dislikes to Mike. In the teachers' lounge he had voiced the opinion that "he couldn't wait to get his hands on Mike." He had heard his case discussed, of course, and in his opinion it was all a matter of discipline—not academic discipline, but physical punishment. He would put the fear of God into Mike—"by God, if he'd only pull himself together he didn't need to be so messy and sloppy"—ridicule him a bit, and all his problems would vanish. He believed that all Mike needed was a little roughing up. He was quite young and had been an outstanding athlete in his college days, so his ideal was the well-muscled, well-coordinated male, and Mike's clumsiness truly offended him.

I knew that Mrs. Jackson herself was baffled by Mike sometimes to the point of irritation, as we all were. With anyone less cooperative we knew we would lose everything we had gained and never find a solution to his problems.

Before we talked about other possible schools, she had another suggestion as to how to overcome his difficulties in remembering left from right. Next year he would be old enough to join a military drill class where many boys spent their Friday afternoons. Could I think of a better place to get detailed, thorough practice in telling left from right? So Mike joined the Knickerbocker Greys for this—literally—pedestrian reason.

Mrs. Jackson's next recommendation did give me a jolt. Mike should not only be taken out of Collegiate at the end of the year, she emphasized, but should be entered in Saint Bernard's, the school that had the reputation of being the most rigid, the most disciplined in New York. Even conservatives agreed that it was more British than the British school system on which it had been modeled. It had a classical approach to education; masters imported from Oxford, Sandhurst, and Cambridge, French in second grade, Latin in the fifth, algebra in the seventh, a lot of history, no social studies, and—Shakespeare. Birchings too no doubt, I muttered. It did not sound right for Mike.

Mrs. Jackson shrugged me off. There was discipline and discipline. Collegiate was the perfect place for her athletic, extroverted son she pointed out; it was not perfect for Mike. Her boy might or might not fit into Saint Bernard's, but why experiment when he was well-adjusted and happy? Mike was neither—so why *not* experiment—or at least take a look. But

47

it only went through eighth grade, I protested. Take one step at a time, she counseled, Mike was desperately unhappy in school, and his troubles seemed bound to become worse. I shuddered at the thought. If he could not continue his slow improvement, he would be retarded in fact, if not according to his proven intelligence.

Obviously, she was right, there was no harm in looking. I had no right to be so prejudiced when I knew nothing about the school. Besides, Saint Bernard's was what they called "selective." Even in those days there were four candidates for every opening in the school, and only an optimist would envision them eager to take on sloppy, unremarkable Mike, with his mysterious handicap.

The office at Saint Bernard's was very polite, quite formal, and less than enthusiastic when I called, but I did receive an invitation to spend a day visiting the classes.

Saint Bernard's, indeed, was different.

I came into the downstairs hall at the moment that classes were changing. There was the usual noisy, happy stampede, as young male animals took this occasion to get rid of energies pent up from the strain of sitting more or less still for fifty minutes. Changing classes was always a near riot at Collegiate too. But from a room at the side of the hall stepped a wiry figure who rapped loudly on the door frame. Dead silence.

"I do not mind necessary noise," announced a beautifully modulated voice, calculated to carry to the farthest reaches of the top floor, "I do mind an excess, which is going to give me a very bad headache. We will all go back to the classrooms we have just left and try once more to get from class to class without endangering either my hearing or the state of the staircase—which, I do not need to remind you, is rather old."

48

Wow! I thought. Back they went, and the exercise was repeated with proper regard for the ancient staircases and Mr. R.I.W. Westgate's sensibilities.

"Thank you," the head called after the boys' backs, "I believe that I will now be able to get through the day."

Rigid discipline! This was right out of Dickens or Fielding. Some school: some place for Mike! At least I wasn't committed to a full day. I would leave at the first possible minute.

In the first class I visited I was accepted with an ill-concealed lack of enthusiasm. Outside the classroom, Mr. Strange, a small, thin Englishman, made no bones about the fact that he considered any visitor an intrusion, and mothers more than he could be expected to bear with any pretense of patience.

As we entered, the boys rose to their feet as one man. "Good morning, Sir," they chorused. Crochety Mr. Strange escorted me to a chair (well off in a corner of the room), seated me with a ceremony that would have been suitable for Queen Victoria, and announced that Mrs. Clarke was going to be their guest for the period. The young gentlemen stood until I had arranged myself; Mr. Strange had put the text book—opened to the proper place—in my hands, and he had seated himself. He then waved permission to the class to do likewise.

I could see that it was going to be a long fifty minutes.

The amenities taken care of, I had time to case the classroom—as they say—something was puzzlingly different, and that something was the lack of clutter. There were no outer garments, no books and notes and skates piled in odd corners. Furthermore, when a boy frantically pawed through his desk and then waved "Sir, Sir" and announced that his homework and pencils were elsewhere, Mr. Strange remarked serenely that desks were supplied as depositories for such tools and the young man had been given ample time before class to attend to the matter. He was not to distract his classmates with his plight.

With no more ado, the lessons began. The boys raised their hands for permission to speak and, since there were black marks for forgetting to address the master either by his full name or "Sir," the boys sensibly had reduced all the teachers to the safe common denominator of "Sir."

The lesson was in algebra and seemed advanced for seventh graders. But, almost imperceptibly, in the midst of all this starchiness something was happening, that even a determinedly prejudiced person like myself could not ignore. "Sir, Sir, Sir," a boy would call frantically from the back. Soon the air was blue with Sirs, and waving arms, and *excitement*.

"Sir" had completely forgotten me and had been transformed into a gnome as spirited as the boys themselves. He laughed with them, and taunted them on their own level, and they answered right back. The decibel level was higher, if anything, than back at Collegiate, and made the slapjack whiners seem absolutely inhibited. Yet there was none of the disorganized pandemonium, the nonlearning process which one would have expected in this distinctly nonrarefied, non-stiff-upper-lip atmosphere. I became fascinated. Mr. Strange was obviously and skillfully directing a performance whose ending was known to him alone, and in the process the boys were pushing him to teach them. Like a good director, he was never out of control.

I doubt that any of his boys will ever forget his formula for finding the height of a flagpole by using the shadow it cast.

"First you take this cat," he began conversationally, "a splendidly educated cat, to be sure. It climbs to the top of the pole and lets down a string . . ."

The nonsense and the lesson went on, and when the fifty minutes were over I felt cheated. What enchanting new animal was Mr. Strange going to pluck from his straggly beard tomorrow?

At the lesson's end, he threw an eraser in the general direction of a boy who had been particularly dense, and cheerfully reminded the boy who had forgotten pencil and notebooks that there would be dire consequences if his memory failed again on the morrow. In the few minutes' grace before the bell rang for next class, I decided one thing. Antimother, though he was, Mr. Strange genuinely liked boys and loved teaching. And the boys liked him, sarcasm and flying erasers included. They crowded around him, laughing and exchanging body punches among themselves, while he looked on, pleased and benign. They did not need to relax on the stairs, although I was to learn that that scene was part of the calculated entertainment. Mr. Strange dismissed me with a courtly bow. He did not pretend to like mothers any more after class than before.

I stayed my allotted time; Mr. Strange's cat could not have dragged me away. I disapproved in principle of the school caps and jackets, the air thick with "Sirs," but after seeing three other classes at different levels I had to admit that I had never seen so many boys going about the business of getting an education so willingly.

I came downstairs for my talk with the headmaster with very divided feelings, and I said so.

The head agreed placidly that mine was a usual reaction; Saint Bernard's never seemed to be precisely what visitors imagined it would be. Many times—it seems—the visitor walked out expressing outright condemnation. Saint Ber-

51

nard's, he noted, did not coddle its boys. The two recreation periods in the yard were very rough as I might have noticed. I had noticed. If parents wanted their boys coddled either physically or academically, Saint Bernard's, for its part, was not sure it wanted to bother with them. In the meantime, there were certain, unbreakable rules; within their pale, the boys had practically perfect freedom.

The head suggested that my husband bring Mike over—mothers were fine for advance spying, but from then on it was a strictly masculine transaction. For my part, I felt that—in fairness—I must outline Mike's puzzling learning problems and explain that while Collegiate was a completely reputable institution, it had not seemed the place for Mike. I told him about the testing and told him that the results would be available to him should he care to see them.

Mr. Westgate listened intently. He asked many questions, some of which seemed irrelevant at the time. He was as interested in Mike's lack of sense of direction, as he was in his spelling and writing difficulties. He told me he had heard of boys with similar problems; he did not know what to do about them specifically, but he said that he would rather work with a bright boy with problems than a mediocre clod whom he would be expected to shoehorn into his father's preparatory school. Naturally, he would make no commitment either way until he had talked with Mike.

Mike's father liked the headmaster; he found him cultured, interesting, and not at all stodgy. We began to wonder . . . why not? Mike was having a bad time at the school we had thought best for him. It would have suited his father, but Mike was not his father.

Mike spent a day at the school, going to classes, joining in the activities, and being observed by the headmaster, the masters, and—in the background—the remedial teacher, surprisingly in this determinedly masculine atmosphere, a very charming woman. We had agreed that if Mike came home and said he hated the place, that would have to be that, but Mike came home beaming. Mr. Strange had shown him a marvelous new system where numbers and symbols actually did what you wanted them to do. Out in the park and in the yard, there were games and teams for everyone, and it did not seem to make any difference which you chose—"Never mind, there must be something you can do." Mike's contribution, as a visitor, was to stand on his head longer than anyone else in the gym period. This it seemed, was as important as catching a ball. It was the first happy day he had spent in a school.

# CHAPTER

Saint Bernard's *was* very British and made no apologies for it. The headmaster considered that the English had evolved the best form of education and there was no need to dump it in Boston harbor with the tea. Collegiate's democracy was well known, but we were agreeably surprised to find that—with a minimum of fanfare—the students at Saint Bernard's represented the same cross section of backgrounds. There was the same proportion of scions of old New York families, the new rich, sons of struggling writers and artists, and some boys who were plain poor. The ratio of scholarship boys was identical with Collegiate: twenty percent. There the resemblance ended. There was the all-important difference in size—ten or twelve boys to a class—the academic approach, and the attitude toward sports: all of prime importance where Mike was concerned.

The differences began with the number of grades. There were fourteen instead of the conventional eight. Ideally, a boy skipped one each year until the seventh grade. On the other hand a boy could move up a single notch and not feel left behind—with the resulting bruising of his ego—since no grade was ever repeated. It was a very fluid system. The boy who had skipped a grade could move back to that halfway square without opprobrium if the lessons seemed too much for him, and anytime during the year a boy could move upward if he was doing well. On one memorable occasion, an entire class changed places, A descending to B, while B became A.

Parents were frequently heard to grumble that they did not know what grade their boy was in, by conventional standards, but that was the idea. Nowadays educators use the term "unstructured" to reflect the philosophy, if not the methods. Saint Bernard's had established a prototype of the open schoolroom so much admired today. There were definite, even rigid rules, as I had been told on my first visit and the most important was the one stating that a boy was not to distract his classmates from the lesson in hand. The rights of the class as a whole took precedence over the whims or exuberance of the individual.

While a tendency to overneatness was considered not quite manly, order was something else again. Books were to be kept in place, notebooks at the ready, homework handed in on time and no excuses. Jackets, shirts, and ties, were worn at all times. The jackets might be tattered, the shirts less than immaculate, and the ties hand-me-downs, but the idea seemed to be that any let-down in the way of sloppiness could contribute to intellectual goofing off. It was not a church school, but no one of any faith or lack of it was excused from morning prayers. The headmaster considered that to rule otherwise would leave a boy culturally deprived, with no foundation for the countless allusions to religion in both classical and popular books.

If "Sir" was to keep control of his production, he needed to emphasize his position as director at the beginning of each performance—hence the standing until permission was given to be seated. Within this framework, the paradox could be accomplished; as the headmaster had told me, the boys could be given a freedom that would have been impossible if there had been no rules. The system was designed to create a climate for learning. A bored, inattentive boy did not fit into this atmosphere, while a disruptive one was not allowed to disrupt.

"I am a teacher, not a policeman," one master remarked coldly to a father who complained that his boy had been sent home to stay until he was ready to appreciate the advantages offered in his particular classroom.

Saint Bernard's was not every boy's cup of tea, as the headmaster had warned us, but fortunately for us—although we could not know it at the time—the system he advocated is now considered the best workable and possibly the only one for the Mikes of this world, despite the fact that the problems faced by dyslexics were hardly taken into consideration when the school was established. Asking a child like Mike to decide when to study, and what, and how, takes time from the necessary fundamental training. Being part of the decision-making process may be splendid practice for the well-adjusted quick learner, but it can only lead to more confusion for the already confused.

The system demanded as much of the teachers as it did of their pupils. There was not a teachers' training credit among the thirty instructors at Saint Bernard's. They were expected to be experts in their specialized subject; to follow what Robert Frost has called the fundamental rule for good teachers: "A teacher begins by loving his subject and ends by loving his students." Or as it was stated at Saint B's: "Oral teaching is best for education and culture. . . . A maximum of instruction and a minimum of books."

I have tried to outline the school atmosphere that helped Mike to relax and begin to be able to learn. Saint Bernard's was to do for Mike what swimming had done for him as a small boy, building up his self-image as a person who could perform among his peers. He was not a failure, a dullard, or retarded, and the system bolstered that opinion. The emotional climate was as conducive to mental health as the academic climate was to learning.

The headmaster himself decided to stay after school to deal with Mike's horrible handwriting. It was a labor of love and more an exercise in art, since each stroke was made as a unity in itself. After a year, so long as Mike could take up to ten minutes per page, his handwriting was clear but immature, resembling that of a facile eight-year-old. In the ordinary way of putting pencil to paper, there was little improvement, but he did learn the mechanics of forming letters, and reinforced the image of them in his own mind. He also had remedial reading and spelling three times a week with the charming Mrs. Leistikow. His reading enjoyment was not spoiled by being stopped for bits and pieces of grammar or spelling, but his diction was corrected when he read aloud. He became more and more skilled in digesting and summarizing the sense of the pages, even if he could neither spell nor pick out the individual words. His teacher was pleased; she had been hired to make certain her boys grasped the meaning of a subject, not just the words. At the end of the sixth grade, Mike was reading in advance of his class level.

Spelling methods went right back to the eighteen-nineties. The small worn spelling book spelled the word "back" by having a boldface **B** followed by a space then *ack;* "Deck" was boldface **D**; space; sound out *eck*.

Mike knew his alphabet and studied the words phonetically. He began to recognize individual words and to spell three- and four-letter ones correctly. He also started French, with the predicated result: he was now dyslexic in both English and French.

Latin was the first language that gave him something to hold onto. It was logical, like math. You learned the rule for the ablative absolute, and knew that all ablative absolutes would always be formed in the same way. Letters always had the same sounds. Nouns and verbs were found in the same place in sentences. Endings for first declension nouns never changed suddenly and you always knew where you were with second conjugation verbs. (Dr. Alex D. Bannantyne, an international authority in dyslexia therapy, has devised a method of teaching the dyslexic using Latin prefixes as memory-joggers. For example, *com* or *con* (from *cum*) can be counted on to connote that the word itself will have a meaning which must be followed by the understood—if unvoiced—"with." Latin stems have the same stability.

But it was not until he met Mr. Strange and his talented cat in seventh grade that Mike found his true vocation. He became so fascinated with algebra that there came a day, in English class, when it was noticed that he was indulging in a

58

pastime popular among school boys; he was reading a more delectable tidbit, cleverly inserted inside his Enslish text. When the teacher pounced on him, he was faced with an unusual dilemma: Mike was not reading a comic book, he was working through a set of supplementary algebra teasers loaned him by Mr. Strange.

If I could explain why Mike could excel at Latin and be at the top of his class in algebra while still making mistakes in fourth grade arithmetic, I would command the attention of an international congress of experts. The reason why dyslexic children tend to be exceptionally gifted in these disciplines is a continuing mystery. As we have noted, Einstein was unable to do simple arithmetic when he propounded the theory of relativity.

Despite his aversion to English, Mike was accepted as a bright boy, with problems to be taken in their stride by adult teachers. They, too, learned "Mike-ese" as one would learn a foreign language. There was enough of a pattern in his reversals of letters and syllables, there were enough similarities in the ways he formed his $a$'s or $g$'s or $r$'s that they managed to get through his written work, even if it was an unwelcome struggle.

Since no one knew what caused his idiosyncracies, this acceptance was what Mike needed most. Discounting his poor speech and written work, he was doing well. He was learning and not piling up the frustrations and despairs of academic failure that certainly would have been his lot in a big bustling public or private school. The same held true in athletics. As Mike had said when he came home from his visit, there was a first, second, and third team in everything. If a boy did not make it in team sports, he boxed, or fenced, or did fancy acrobatics. Mike liked boxing, for unlike games with balls, there was no need to judge the speed of a flying object, no confusion between left and right.

The school paper once printed that Saint Bernard's had been "unjustly maligned, as a rough school where a boy had to learn to take it." It was, however, a rough school, and teachers breathed a sigh of relief after every recess when there was no greater mayhem than a few bruises and a bloody nose.

On the day a treble-voiced six-year-old arrived, he learned the school's attitude through the old school song:

> *I never seem to make a team,*
> *My name's unknown to fame,*
> *The captain's list my name has missed. . . .*
> *But still I play the game.*

The teachers too lived by the rule. One young coach saw that Mike was never going to do much in his particular area—basketball—but his job was to turn out boys with some experience in team sports, so instead of leaving him to kick his heels in a corner, he gave Mike extra coaching where he could use both hands. Patiently, he had Mike stand on the free throw line, and throw the ball through the hoop over and over again. It was thanks to him that Mike tasted triumph one afternoon. Saint Bernard's was playing Collegiate, and when, close to the end of the game the score was tied, Saint Bernard's was given two free throws. The coach signaled Frank Merriwell—or rather, Mike—to make the attempts. He did: two perfect baskets. It did much to make up for those winters of frustration at his old alma mater.

The spirit of good sportsmanship advocated by the school song, carried over into academic matters. The school had two honor rolls, the usual one for high grades, and a second, "highly commended," to single out extraordinary effort on the part of less talented boys. Mike was commended for his handwriting!

Possibly Saint Bernard's most important contribution to Mike and his fellows lay in not forgetting that they were boys. The assistant headmaster—the erudite Mr. Fry—might translate poetry from the Greek for his own amusement, but he did not expect similar flights of scholarship from thirteen-year-olds. In fact, as he looked over the dry-as-dust history texts, he decided that he would be bored to tears with every one of them. The result was *Fry's History of the English Speaking Peoples,* a mimeographed text book for the eighth grade. Mike may be weak on dates, and he would probably misspell the names of the principals, but he can still fight the Battle of Agincourt in detail. That year, under Mr. Fry's tutelage, Mike discovered the delight of reading for fun. (The Department of Health, Education and Welfare now postulates the theory of *Overteach:* that children be drilled in reading until they are able to enjoy the printed word. That same Dr. Bannantyne said that to give the dyslexic the skills to read and then not to continue until he *loves* to read deprives him of his rights.) Mr. Fry accomplished this miracle not by pouring more "classics" over the heads of his boys, but by rewarding good behavior and extra efforts by reading aloud old-fashioned, rousing narrative poems, such as *How They Brought the Good News from Ghent to Aix,* and as a special treat he would give his own rendition of *The Prisoner of Zenda,* a performance that would have graced any stage.

Mike did most of his studying in school, but each weekend brought the traumatic moment for the English essay that had to be handed in on Monday morning. At the last possible moment on Sunday afternoons, Mike would sit himself down

61

to his pencil-chewing. Half the time I could not read what he had put down, and there were times when he was not sure himself. Feeling very devious and guilty—at least I did—we hit on a scheme. Mike would dictate his compositions to me, I would take them down on the typewriter just as he spoke them, and he would copy them back from the typescript. There did not seem to be any better way to cope with written English, as far as Mike was concerned.

Toward the end of seventh grade, Mike was watching me type, and later that night he got out the typewriter and began picking out the letters for himself. By the beginning of eighth grade he had taught himself a workable peck-and-go system, and we bought him his own typewriter. "I'm never going to be able to write so you can read it—face it, mom."

It seemed to us as the final year began that Mike was all but cured of whatever ailed him. He read and understood what he was reading, never mind how he saw the letters. He was spelling simple words. He could not write legibly at a normal speed, but he had his typewriter. He had savored his moment on the basketball court, and he had learned left from right well enough to become a lieutenant in the Greys and to bicycle on country roads in the summer.

Then a series of episodes that seemed trifling individually came together, and Mike's life began to fall apart again. There was the small tragedy of his tooth. Mike—who couldn't carry a tune and was denied the privilege of taking piano-lessons—had learned to play a recorder. He became good enough to warrant a secondhand clarinet for Christmas. He was just beginning to make bearable noises on it, when the hearty masculine recess at school took its toll. One day as Mike was trying to catch a baseball—a front tooth was knocked out, and he and the clarinet parted company forever. His disappointment was very real and very deep. I myself was unintentionally responsible for the other incidents that compounded his disintegration. We rarely paid much attention to Mike's efforts in shop, because he was all thumbs and never brought home those carefully polished bookends to be put in a place of honor. One night, however, he arrived with his eyes shining, breathless under the weight of a huge contraption, some four feet long and three feet high. He put it down in the middle of the living-room floor and looked around for approval.

"Wh-what is it?" I asked.

"An ice boat," Mike replied, scornful of my ignorance. "See, it has the two planing rudders. See, I've welded the steel right on the wood and Sir says it's a splendid job. And here's the tiller and the mast, and you run the sails up here. . . ."

I could also see where he had dented the steel, and all the small holes where he had experimented. Even if it was seaworthy it was not practical. Stupidly, I forgot that this unattractive vehicle was the first thing Mike had ever made with his own two hands.

"But what earthly good is it?" I asked, "You couldn't sail it across a goldfish pond."

The iceboat disappeared and was never mentioned again.

My next contribution was equally devastating. After yet another long, family session, we had decided that Mike would probably do better if he went away to school. Aside from the fact that all city high schools—private and public—tend to be large and impersonal, there are the numerous distractions offered by the city itself. If Mike, at this point, did not need the freedom to decide between English and slapjack, he certainly would not be able to deal with the freedom to decide between a Saturday at the movies, a Friday night dance, and a Sunday afternoon goofing off, instead of a session with his books.

I was quite aware of the fact that—without editing—Mike was capable of spelling "apple" "apel," "apil," and "paple" all on the same page. Boarding school would not be Saint Bernard's. Would a higher level school bother with this nonsense about Mike's disability, we wondered anxiously?

I felt increasingly guilty, for I was aware that this state of affairs was partly my fault. During the years I acted as secretary for his compositions I had neither altered his sentence structure or his thoughts, but I had corrected the spelling before he copied the pages out. I thought the system was working, for Mike was picking out more and more words correctly on the typewriter. It never occurred to me that this might not have anything to do with my contribution. But I did realize that now he was going away there would be no crutch to lean on, and the deception would be uncovered.

I over-reacted. Sunday afternoons began to look like a movie chase, with me pursuing Mike around the house from room to room, pencil and paper in hand, scolding, making him look up words in the dictionary, determined he would learn to spell properly before the term was over.

The atmosphere grew so tense that Mike's father finally suggested that all this nagging wasn't going to get Mike anywhere. I replied that it wasn't my idea of a way to spend a Sunday afternoon either, but did he have any better suggestions? No, he did not, but neither did he approve of this particular act.

Mike retreated to his room with his newly acquired bongo drums. He became obsessed by them, pounding them endlessly, not with accompanying records, but beating out his own jerky rhythms for hours on end, in an insistent repetitious maddening pattern, until I would beg, "Please, Mike, how about a little quiet for a change?"

No one guessed how tense Mike had become—nor that he was attempting to work it out on the drums—until the day of the Secondary Education Tests in January (the S.E.T.'s are junior college boards taken by eighth graders to determine whether the child is boarding school material). Mike came home from his tests, flung himself on his bed, and cried for the first time since he was six. His head was buried in his pillow, and he responded to any questions we put to him by shaking his head through the sobs. Neither his father nor I could imagine what had happened.

Finally he raised a tear-stained face.

"I failed the S.E.T.'s," he announced, "and now I can't get into boarding school, and that means I won't get to go to college, and that means I'm going to be a failure." Back down into the pillow went his head and he shook with more sobs.

We comforted him by assuring him that he could always go somewhere else and college was almost five years away. At last he stopped crying and consented to eat a hamburger, but he remained gloomy. We were worried, and called the school to see whether they shared Mike's apprehension. The headmaster, Mr. Westgate, assured me that academically they did not. He promised that he and the other teachers would be as reassuring as possible when Mike appeared, and he thanked me for calling. He wanted to see me and my husband, and I could not help recalling that ominous interview years ago when we were told that Mike was retarded. Were Mike's tears another symptom?

Mr. Westgate was cautious, but concerned. He had been watching Mike closely because some of the teachers had reported that he seemed too tense. They thought he might be working too hard; "over-achieving" was the term in those days. There were other signs of strain, too, his handwriting was deteriorating—if such a thing were possible—and although his grades were still good, they were afraid that Mike might be paying too high a price.

Mr. Westgate knew what a struggle the learning process had been for Mike; how hard and with what determination he had worked over the past four years. Had those years, he wondered, taken their toll in a nervous breakdown?

He told us that the school maintained a close relationship with a doctor who had been successful in helping other boys in the school over emotional rough spots. He had toyed with the idea that all of Mike's troubles might be psychological in origin, and that therapy might clear up the lot. Now would be the time—especially in light of these warning signals—to seek out expert advice before the strains of adolescence were added.

This was upsetting, but nothing like the shock we had received during the Collegiate interview. Nevertheless, we were not well prepared to accept that Mike was emotionally disturbed and about to be sent to a psychiatrist, with all its connotations.

Another preconceived notion was about to be shattered there. The doctor was a woman—a psychologist not a psychiatrist—married, and with children of her own. Dr. Edith Taglicht Schmidt was so round and rosy and motherly, one would have guessed her profession to be that of school nurse or housemother. She did not have much of an office, she certainly did not have a couch, and there was not enough of a desk to lean across. She explained to us that every child had troubles during puberty. It was normal; in fact she believed a

66

child without any troubles would be a very dull creature. The difference here, she pointed out, was one of degree. For some, the problems were sufficiently overpowering to interfere with the learning process. Right now, she was talking with a number of boys from Saint Bernard's who seemed to need help. Among her other attributes, she possessed the most soothing voice in the world, and after listening to her for twenty minutes I was certain everything was going to be all right.

Her methods were interesting. There was no recognizable therapy involved. She tutored the children in whatever lesson or book or subject he brought along to her—it could be math, English, or a language—and while they grappled with the lessons together, the child talked about many things: the classroom, his teacher, his friends, parents, and siblings. At the end of a month or so, Dr. Schmidt could make a very shrewd evaluation of her pupil—she never called him a patient—his family environment, and what was troubling him.

Several weeks later, Dr. Schmidt felt that Mike's reading and writing difficulties might stem from a lack of left-right dominance. He was a middle child, and although tall and well-filled-out now, he had been undersized and spindly and had felt even more so emotionally. There were deficiencies in the home atmosphere, such as the inevitable conflicts between husband and wife, which would be better remedied.

She believed that the strain of overcoming his learning difficulties plus the changes and pressures of dawning adolescence, had brought into the open emotions and questions that Mike had repressed since babyhood. This was often the case, Dr. Schmidt assured us. She thought she could help him to "talk them out of his system" by June.

Certainly, those afternoons helped. Mike grew less tense,

and the bongo drumming became more reasonable, both in time and tone. Mr. Westgate noticed a difference at school, and we congratulated ourselves that we had faced a possible problem head on, and stopped its progress before it got started. Mike was ready to take the step into boarding-school life and a world that did not revolve around him.

For his part, Mike became quite fond of his "teacher"—the children never called her anything else—and years later, in a dark moment when he was a college sophomore, he instinctively turned to her, and only to her for help and encouragement.

Now the choice of schools had to be made. In spite of his forebodings, Mike had passed those S.E.T.'s. The headmaster agreed to recommend him for whatever school he liked. So we made the circuit, feeling a little like Goldilocks confronted by the three chairs, one big school, one middle-sized one and one small one. Mr. Westgate, we knew, favored the small one, for he did not think Mike was ready to cope with an Exeter or an Andover any better than he was suited to the *laissez-faire* of Collegiate. However, he thought Mike should see the difference in schools of various sizes, and must have a voice in the final decision.

Mike was no help. He thought all of them just dandy so we applied to three, fairly certain that our choice would be made for us by a process of elimination. Mike was accepted by all of them!

After we had seen the school the headmaster favored, we knew that it was our choice, too. It was small, warm, and friendly, but again, we were not the ones who would be going there. As the week in which he would have to make up his mind drew to a close, Mike's basketball coach happened to be in the park while Mike was walking the dog. Whether it was a coincidence or not, we shall never know, but . . .

"Want to throw a couple of balls?" he asked. Mike could catch the balls Mr. Beebe threw. He tied the dog to the fence and they exchanged a couple of desultory throws and catches.

"Decided where you're going next year?" asked Mr. Beebe.

Mike said he had not.

"Got a choice?"

Mike mentioned his choices.

"Great schools, all of them," admitted the coach, "but why don't you go to Groton? Too many big guys go to the other two. Lots of them wait after they get out of high school and have a year of post grad. first. Their teams play college freshmen, but I think you'd make a team at Groton."

And so Mike himself selected the small, pleasant school where he would spend the next four years. Essentially it was to be another period of insulation against the competition of the world itself. But Mike was still in the larval stage, still struggling toward a mature shape and image.

The week of graduation from Saint Bernard's approached, heralded by a minor family crisis. Peter was quite sick—with measles—so I decided that my place was at home with him. Then I got a call from the office at Mike's school. It was the headmaster himself, and he told me, crisply and firmly, that Peter could do without me for an hour or two since there was someone else with him, but I must not miss graduation. Something special was going to happen.

I tried to think what could be all that special. Mike might just get the award as "boy who has worked hardest and made progress in the face of difficulties" but this was something of a left-handed honor.

69

The day dawned, and ceremony and prizes went on and on: Mike got the math prize, which did not seem like a particularly good reason for that phone call. Finally came the last, highest prize to "the boy, who by his actions and spirit has shown himself in every way the highest product of the school . . . Michael Clarke."

In the language of today, this was where it was at for Saint Bernard's. Mike was not the best student but he had managed to rank fifth in the class. He was not the best athlete, and had captained no teams, but he had gone out for every sport; he had tried harder. He had no lead in the class play, but painfully, syllable by phonetically-learned syllable, he had mastered the few lines allotted the Tailor in *The Taming of the Shrew*, and they had rung out loud and true on the night of the play. He had done his best.

Mike—clumsy, inarticulate, funny, but oh-so-serious Mike —stepped down from the ceremonial handshake completely dazed, clutching the cup to his chest. As we left that noon, Mr. Westgate looked after the retreating figure of Mike.

"There's a hard nut to crack," he said approvingly.

It was his crowning accolade.

# CHAPTER

# 6

From Mike's class history at Groton:

"Clarke . . . arrived with everything he owned packed neatly in a garbage pail. . . ." This was the judgment of hindsight. It took Mike a year and a half to establish the distinction of being the messiest, sloppiest boy in the school.

On the surface, the boarding school years continued the pattern begun at Saint Bernard's. Both schools had a common goal: to establish a "climate for learning." In practice, Groton was a preparation for the real world, completing the transition from supervised freshmen in the study hall to virtually unregulated senior, sharing with the faculty the responsibility of maintaining discipline among the younger boys.

Books "exposing" Eastern boarding schools, have been frequent and popular. Mike's father and I had read about the snob-factories that were stultifying intellectually, presided over by loutish, bored, and boring teachers; inhabited by rich, spoiled kids, with their expensive cars, astronomical allowances—"you mean you only get fifty dollars a week?" — and the high and wide weekends in New York or Boston.

There are such schools, of course, but Groton was not one of them. No radios were allowed, because radios can distract others; there was no smoking, because the headmaster and the school doctor considered it unhealthy; allowances were held at one dollar a week—a boy did not need more since there were no weekend passes—classes being scheduled through six days, with only Saturday afternoon free. At that time, unless there was a football or baseball game, boys were free to walk the two miles to the village where an ice cream soda might be negotiated. Until senior year there was a "lights out" time; possession of liquor in any form at any time meant expulsion. That was all, as long as a boy kept his grades up.

Which is not to say that high spirits were not expected, indeed they were secretly approved. The most proudly cherished escapades were both outrageous and puerile. So long as they were not dangerous to mind or body the school took a great deal in its stride. The Rector of Groton knew that boys under sixteen have to goof off on occasion, and better be silly than sorry. It was a system calculated to deal with tensions within an acceptable framework.

Each class had its genius who knew enough about electricity and circuits to construct an illicit radio, and the satisfaction of mission accomplished was permitted; confiscation took place next day. Doorways were routinely booby-trapped, and the only mother to be enshrined in school myth was the one who helped her son pie the beds of an entire dormitory—with frogs!

Extracurricular imagination was dealt with logically. When Mike's class wet down every towel in the gym for a smashing game of cracking them at each other, the gym teacher happened by, surveyed the mess, and walked out again, assigning the boys to continuing throwing towels at each other for the next three hours. Wet towels are very heavy. It can be said in favor of this system that the boys did not miss binges in the city.

Once accepted by the school, a boy was accepted by everyone in it. A boy on scholarship had as much opportunity to be voted class president as anyone else. Behind the great iron gates, no one—literally—gave a damn for the pecking order of the outside world. The highest honor of the school—that of being one of the senior prefects—was given to a black student, and it was taken for granted that he should attend all the dances and parties. This was in the late fifties, remember. In Mike's class, highest scholastic honors went to a young black man from Africa, who possibly passed on more education to the boys in the school than he received.

Of course this atmosphere did not prepare young blacks for the discrimination they would meet at college and in the world. Neither did it prepare Mike for the intellectual discrimination that was to be his lot in later years; but it gave all of them an important feeling of security that saw them through their formative years, as well as a superb education to help them lick the system in the end.

Mike's studies persisted in the familiar worrisome puzzle. When some new device would make its appearance on the academic scene and a breakthrough was anticipated that would set him on the right road, it would eventually be proved useless in his case and Mike would be back where he started.

Fortunately he was not alone in his reading difficulties. There were enough boys with problems—whether they were caused by defective eyesight or neurological disorders—for the school to buy the newest and most expensive machines to correct reading problems. One of these was reputed to do wonders in eye-retraining; sentences were flashed on a screen, from left to right, syllable by syllable, in a dark room, and the boys chanted them aloud as they copied them out.

There were first-rate laboratories at Groton—there had been none at Saint Bernard's—and Mike discovered a second vocation toward which math had been the first step. He found that he could achieve the step-by-step processes of intricate experiments and follow them through to the correct conclusions. His first science courses were in chemistry, but he showed the same brilliance in biology and physics. Small wonder that the science teacher could not believe that Mike had a language disability and took up the "if you would only try harder" refrain that would eventually drive Mike into a near breakdown. Mr. Field was incapable of understanding how a boy so attuned to scientific research, who grasped the concept of its disciplines and logic so quickly, could be so careless, messy, and sloppy in its presentation. He was as convinced as that Collegiate fifth grade teacher that before the four years were over, he could shame, scold, or coax Mike into the neat patterns his experiments showed.

Mike was now old enough to seem to take it in his stride, for on the other hand, he *was* Mr. Field's prize pupil. Since Mr. Field showered him with praise and encouragement Mike tended to brush off his exhortations toward neatness as one of those quirks a boy comes to expect from teachers.

Mr. Field was certain that Mike had a career in the sciences ahead of him, and therefore insisted that he learn German, so Mike made his still mysterious reversals in yet a third language, which—any German student will agree—is reversed enough already. Again, he learned to read German by his particular osmosis without learning to pronounce or spell the words, and the German master soon came to share the science teacher's opinion that Mike was mispronouncing for the sole purpose of outraging his Prussian sense of precision. Mike's German papers fairly bristled with red, green and blue comments about Mike's refusal to "live up to his potentials."

For their own convenience and sanity, the teachers again took the best possible course for Mike, with no idea that they were contributing to his salvation. He was allowed to type all his papers except his formal examinations. Looking back over these compositions, I can see the expected reversals and misspellings, but certainly not as many as in the handwritten work, and it is at least possible to guess at most of the words.

On one term paper of some twenty-four pages, each page contains eight or nine misspellings and reversals. Mike got an A- on the paper: "Quite good; a mature essay that reflects the large amount of work. . . ." Mike was given the knowledge that his efforts had not been glossed over unread, and that particular paper came back with three pages of comments: "On page 20 . . . I like the continuing argument that you cited on page 14 . . . page 19 seems a little unfair to Wilson." It was a tremendous morale builder, even when the comments sputtered into "too many omissions of letters or words, errors that could easily have been corrected by proofreading. . . . see distortment, scabble (?), augraments (arguments), seatinor (senator). . . . Do you really mean to say this? . . . good idea, but a phrase left out here."

The teachers still sweated over the blue books, some, venting their annoyance in sarcastic marginal notes. Gradually, they grew accustomed to the cryptograms and learned to read what they, too, called Mike-ese.

As Mike's parents we did not ask for too much. The suspicion that we were lucky to have him in any school at all continued to loom over us. His adolescence was not progressing easily. During his first year at Groton, we had been annoyed to discover that every pair of pants he owned was destroyed in the carnage of a game called knee-football, played on the knees, with a toy ball. But even with the knees in fit condition, Mike could not have taken last year's pants back to school the following September. He could not get into them at all. From the round, charming baby, and the thin, undersized, nervous boy, he had—during the four years of puberty —grown into a full-sized, well proportioned youngster. We had assumed he would stay that way, but not at all. Mike was becoming gross. Again from a class note: "Clarke, whose vast stomach was not to be sated, set out huge quantities of ice cream in his window sill, which he would invariably find melted in the snow." Which did not deter Clarke from restocking his larder with ice cream and every other variety of foodstuff.

He was not just fat, but fat in spots, like a carelessly stuffed sausage bulging in peculiar and unpredictable places. He had started "filling out" over the summer, and I was delighted. But when we visited school late in October, even a mother could see those unproportioned streaks of pure lard.

Back home, I asked our friendly pediatrician a new variation on the same old question. "Perfectly normal for adolescence," he told me cheerfully. "Got to get ready to handle those heavier bones, you know. I'd call it a good sign." It was

76

not, of course.

I had not heard about compensatory overeating then, but surely the pediatrician, the school doctor, or someone should have taken a look, and wondered?

Not even his classmates' teasing curtailed Mike's eating habits. The only positive thing that happened was that during a February thaw the smell of soured ice cream became so overpowering that by popular demand, Mike's outdoor freezer arrangement ended, though his uneven expansion did not. By the following year, we were forced to shop for his pants in the men's department to fit his peculiar form: slender legs, bursting into an incredible behind. Bills for alterations came to as much as the original price of the pants. Mike did not want to discuss his shape or his eating with anyone, not even with his friend and teacher, Dr. Schmidt. Out of desperation and for lack of the slightest idea of what to do, we did what a psychiatrist today would counsel, we let him eat.

During vacation his room was filled with dirty dishes, leftover food, and sticky glasses. There was a period when I refused to enter it, even to change the bed, but Mike was not at all bothered. In the interests of holding down the insect population I had to give in and haul out the dishes and bits and pieces of sandwiches and cake; his study at school must have been revolting.

Once more, the bongo drums began to beat insistently, at all hours (most of them impossible). They sounded like a message sent across some primitive savannah—savage, vibrant, pleading, demanding. "Remember there are people trying to sleep above and below you," I would tell him, and the pounding would stop eventually, but only after a last, defiant series of rolls.

Along with the new urgency of the drums came another

77

change, a personality change. Mike scarcely spoke at all, and when he did it was in a mumble so low it was difficult to catch the words. They were likely to be unpleasant, anyway. He had tantrums about nothing and would bang into his room with such violence that now, years later, plaster will not stick to the walls around the door frame.

As his disposition became more and more unpleasant, the eating stopped as suddenly as it had started. The fanny disappeared and his legs lengthened. He turned against malteds. Personally, I preferred the glutton of the two. Even I could sense that food had been helping him hold the fort against some unmentionable inner devils and unbearable tensions. For all their teasing during the fatso period that lasted into his junior year, none of this turned away the friends of his own age. Through it all—including this new, brooding withdrawal—he was never a loner. In the summers there were the usual girls, and his own particular rat pack was as united in adventure and mischief as ever, so it did not bother us that Mike was not reading or studying during those summers.

At the beginning of Mike's third year, the school noted the change, and became sufficiently concerned to ask Mike's father up for a talk. Several of Mike's teachers had spoken to the headmaster, and he himself had made a point of observing Mike for the past few weeks. It seemed that Mike had now reached the point of taking any measures to avoid speaking to adults. The Mike who used to play fives with the masters, and was best friends with their various dogs who hold tenure in every New England classroom, no longer liked to drop by for a chat and a cookie of an afternoon.

Mike's father could look out of the study door, it was suggested, and see for himself—there went Mike, charging across the oval, his head between his shoulders, looking neither to left or right. Not only did he not speak, he did not answer when spoken to, but the change had been too abrupt for anyone to take umbrage. Mike—everyone was certain—was in some deep, inner turmoil.

His recitations, too, deteriorated into a practically unintelligible mumble, and he became furious if anyone asked him to repeat, almost as if he were a baby gabbling on the beach again.

Our trusty doctor reiterated that Mike seemed to be having a particularly difficult adolescence, but then added that most people did not realize what a hard time all boys went through. Hadn't he thinned down? "Yes," I admitted timidly, but it had seemed to coincide much too frighteningly with this—for the first time I used the term—this withdrawal.

Groton was not as sanguine as the doctor. They felt Mike should go into Boston to consult with the school's psychiatrist. So we met the great man. His desk was so wide and he peered over it through his large glasses so wisely that I was intimidated; but surely, if anyone could decide what was wrong with Mike, we speculated, it would have to be someone with his impressive background.

Mike started journeying to Boston two afternoons a week. The headmaster was certain that talking things over for three or four months would probably straighten him out, but Mike was still going into Boston the winter of his senior year, and there had been little change.

He was no longer sullen, but so quiet and subdued that again the teachers were not sure they preferred this to a more overt reaction. His troubles affected his grades, but not enough to fail, though there would be no high honors, no prizes, no citations at graduation this time, even if he remained respectably in the top quarter of his class—at heaven knows what cost to himself. He even made the football squad. He was still a "hard nut to crack."

It was time to think of college now. We wondered if we could find one small enough to understand Mike, and still give him a respectable education.

Late in October of his senior year, Mike announced casually that he was going to Harvard. Harvard, we queried? Had he visited there?

"No," Mike told us airily. "This guy came down to school and talked to us and *everyone* is going to Harvard." So, of course, he was going with them.

What had Harvard said to him we asked faintly?

They had seen his grades, and had put him down for early acceptance. All he had to do was keep up the grades: "no sweat, mom."

In those days—over ten years ago—there was a system called early acceptance whereby preparatory schools with a good reputation could have their students admitted early to Harvard without the agony of waiting for the May letters, provided, of course, that after admittance the boy did not fail academically, get drunk in public, or otherwise make himself unacceptable.

We thought Mike was taking the whole process too lightly. There must be more to choosing one's college than the fact that a bunch of his buddies from school were going along with him. His headmaster agreed with us emphatically. Once more Mike's father made the trip to Massachusetts.

Dr. Crocker was very, very gloomy, and very, very frank. Once again he took the old line—it sounded like a broken record to us by now—Mike was a fine boy; he had done splendidly at Groton; they were proud of him, the way he had persevered in the face of his handicaps, the way he seemed to

80

be trying to conquer his unfriendliness, or shyness, or whatever it had been. . . . Did we know that he was going to be a house prefect, chosen by the boys? No, he had not told us. However, there remained this mysterious disability, the headmaster pointed out, first appearing in this guise, then in that. This gnawing, unconquered inability to speak clearly, to write legibly, or to spell with fourth grade consistency.

Dr. Crocker seemed to be voicing aloud his own inner worries, his own self-doubts, questioning his own wisdom. Had Groton overprotected Mike? He was splendidly educated. Had Mike told us he had ranked in the top quarter of one percent in the country, in his college board for physics and math? No? Well, he wouldn't, naturally.

He could get through college just as well, Dr. Crocker thought, but not just any college, and certainly not Harvard. Harvard was too large, and too impersonal. Groton had not prepared Mike for a college where there would be no teachers interested in interpreting his speech, or ruining their eyes on his idiosyncratic scribbles. Class recitations at Harvard were of minimal importance, unlike at Groton. At Harvard, grades depended on written papers. He was sorry he had not stopped the interviews and acceptance before they occurred, because Mike's grades made him a natural for Harvard. But without the specifics that had helped him attain them, both his own efforts, and the sympathetic teachers Groton had provided, Harvard was out of the question.

He urged us strongly that Mike go to another small institution, a college of good standing, but one which could give him yet another breather to conquer his disability. Like everyone else, Dr. Crocker was certain Mike would "outgrow it all" given time. Meanwhile, he said flatly: "Mike will flunk out of Harvard, probably the first year."

We all tried to dissuade Mike. We must have been the most unwilling parents and teachers who ever sent a boy off to Cambridge. But now the competitive, stubborn individual that was Mike, stood up to us all and defied us all. He knew he had been babied, and tutored, and coaxed along, he said. He was no fool. It was *his* life, and sometime he was going to have to face up to it, face what the world would say and how it would judge and grade him. He had to know what he was made of, what he was capable of on his own. He was going to find out right now, he insisted, and if he failed it was better to know now than later.

The headmaster reluctantly agreed that he would have to be given his chance. His grades said he could make it, his character said he could make it, and Harvard thought he was going to make it. It was not in the habit of picking freshmen who would fail. We all disagreed with the decision.

At this critical time I made a discovery that led me to hope that, after all these years, we were going to find out what really was the matter with Mike.

# CHAPTER

The first hint that Mike's problems might have a name came from the other side of the Atlantic. The April 1960 issue of *The Independent School Bulletin* listed in its table of contents an article on word blindness by a Miss Edith Norrie, of Denmark. The phrase meant nothing at all to me then, so little that while I was leafing through the magazine I did not even glance at the title page of the article. I was turning to the next page when reproductions of handwriting caught my eye. I froze, and then shook my head, like a swimmer coming out of the surf. "My God," I said aloud, "that's Mike's handwriting!"

There was "London", spelled with a capital *L* that looked

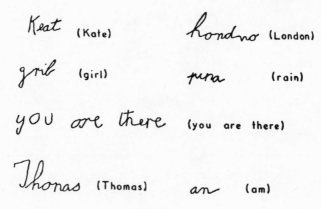

Figure I.

Examples of handwriting which show the reversal of letters,
a difficulty in forming letters, and a confusion of similar but
different letters with one another, typical of people who have
word-blindness (specific language disability — dyslexia).

*This illustration in The Independent School Bulletin
was the first indication I had that Mike's problem had a
name.*

more like a lowercase *h*, the other letters reversed every
which way. There was "Thomas" spelled with an *n*, and
"girl" spelled "grib", with the final *l* a perfectly good *b*. For
one moment I stupidly asked myself how one of Mike's
papers could have found its way to the *Bulletin*.

The caption noted that the examples had been taken from
the writings of several persons, chosen to show the "confusion
of similar but different letters, the reversals and difficulties in
forming letters, typical of people who have word blindness
(specific language disability—dyslexia)."

The term "word blindness" frightened me, while the other
names had no meaning whatsoever, but with the tortured and
cramped calligraphy and bizarre spellings, I was only too fa-

miliar. I turned back and before I had finished reading the first page I realized that here was the explanation of everything that had puzzled and worried us and tormented Mike from his first day at school.

Miss Norrie herself had been a great disappointment to her distinguished father, a famous ophthalmologist, for she had not been able to learn to read or write. She had been allowed to continue at her school, but had done so poorly and had fallen so far behind her class and her age group that at last, she says, "I was forced to leave school without having passed the final examination."

By the age of eighteen, through superhuman effort and self-experimentation, by inventing and discarding devices, and keeping and recording those that were successful, Miss Norrie had taught herself to read, to write on the typewriter, and to speak so that she was understood.

Miss Norrie, still groping, still not understanding what her own disability could be, decided that she would become a speech therapist, as her contribution toward helping others with the mysterious affliction. It was during her training and later professional work that she became aware that there was a specific difficulty, called "word blindness"—a term used to differentiate between persons like herself, and those suffering from alexia, or true brain damage.

It was not until 1936, when Miss Norrie was forty-six, that she felt she knew enough to discuss the whole problem with her father. Miss Norrie was lucky. Not all dyslexics have an ophthalmologist for a father. Neither Dr. Norrie nor his daughter seems to have been aware of the earlier studies of Dr. W. P. Morgan, British ophthalmologist, who in 1896 published the first article describing the condition he called "congenital word blindness."

Father and daughter studied the pattern of Edith's mistakes and the symptoms she had displayed from the time she entered school. Dr. Norrie, who had believed that Edith was brain-damaged, began his own studies, and realized that she was the victim of the lesser known—almost undocumented—dyslexia. Miss Norrie points out that unbeknownst to them this small family conference coincided in time with the studies that Dr. Samuel T. Orton had begun to publish in the United States. Fortunately for scientific research, the family was an established one, and old letters and other documents were available. It became evident that the disability had been passed down through Miss Norrie's mother, and the symptoms of word blindness were traced back for five generations.

Miss Norrie then enlarged the scope of both her studies and her operations. The result was the founding of the Word-Blind Institute, of which she became the first director. She was able to engage in much firsthand research, with both the Danish and British children who were sent to her school, for the redoubtable Miss Norrie had taught herself English.

Miss Norrie also documented cases of dyslexia in German- and French-speaking pupils when other researchers thought the disability was confined to the Danish and English languages. She discovered that the mistakes were identical in character, no matter what the language, so she decided that her chart of symptoms could be used universally for diagnosis, even if it must be adapted for therapy. For example, she noted that many therapists never could understand how a child was incapable of reading a word as a whole even after he had managed to spell it through, letter by letter. The dyslexic child might not comprehend the word as a whole, for—as with Mike—even though he might have a good vocabulary he would not be able to spell or pronounce any of the words in it.

The result—so obvious now—is that the word-blind child may have to read a paragraph or passage over several times, before it makes sense. This can slow down his test performance to such an extent that the verdict of the unknowing would be severe retardation or subnormal intelligence.

In the late nineteen-forties, when Miss Norrie was doing much of her significant pioneering, she herself distinguished between the word-blind and the word-deaf; the former have perfect hearing—in that the sounds come through loud and clear—but they register in a jumble. A person could be afflicted with one, without the other, she felt mistakenly. However, she found enough cases where her pupils were both word-blind and word-deaf to justify including auditory therapy in her method, since if one heard a word incorrectly and could never see the word, the difficulties would be more than doubled.

Miss Norrie's system for the education of the word-blind is the Rosetta Stone for present day therapies. Its basic foundation—with various modifications and refinements—is still in use under a variety of names. The method will be described fully in the chapter on education. Briefly, Miss Norrie's system depends on boxes of letters arranged phonetically, instead of alphabetically, with different colors for different sounds. Given a sentence by his instructor, the pupil learns to build his own words, at the same time reinforcing his memory by speaking the letter, and watching how the sound is produced by his tongue and lips in a small mirror.

We realize now that Miss Norrie could not have written as she did, with the depth of feeling and understanding she contributed to the worldwide study of the subject, if she had not been incapacitated herself. She herself had been dismissed as retarded; she had suffered all the emotional problems; she knew the disappointments and frustrations, and their inevitable results. She herself had been defeated, had been rebuffed and humiliated by parents, teachers, and her contemporaries.

She spoke from experience when she wrote of the agony of trying harder and harder to turn in a well-written paper on a subject about which one may know every salient fact, with muscles growing increasingly more tense, the signals to the brain weakening, until the only strength left is to think about *how* one is writing instead of being able to concentrate on *what* one is writing. And back the paper would come, marked "messy; ill-thought out; poorly constructed." I read on. This, Miss Norrie commented, rather grimly, was when the child was lucky. More often the comment would be verbal: "stupid, lazy, careless, messy."

Miss Norrie was the first to document the very real possibility of suicide among dyslexics. The daily defeats, the harsh, uncalled-for judgments, can be disastrous for these sensitive, intelligent children. Every year Miss Norrie discovered children sitting alone, withdrawn from their world, wondering how they could end their unbearable lives. Several actually attempted suicide.

My immediate reaction to the article was to sit down at my desk and write to Miss Norrie. I told Mike's story, what we had done and not done, what he had and had not accomplished, and ended with the fears that all of us felt for him in the larger, less protective environment of the college he was determined to attend. Was it too late? Was there any place here where he might be helped, I asked? After I had sent off the letter—the envelope bulged as though it contained a fullblown manuscript—I was abashed at my temerity. Miss Norrie was famous. She was a very busy, overworked consultant. She was no longer young; at seventy-one she was retired from the Institute she had headed. Realistically, there was only a very slim chance of receiving an answer.

Yet, in spite of all these years of consultations, tests, tutoring, and analyzing, no one at anytime had mentioned that there existed a condition such as this, or held out the hope that there might be a cure. No—that was not the word—for Miss Norrie had made clear that it was not a disease that could be cured, but a malfunction that required rehabilitation and retraining of whatever reflexes were accountable. If she did not answer, where could we turn? I got an answer by return mail. It was a warm, heartfelt letter, typed by Miss Norrie herself in English, with enough letters reversed and left out to endear her to me forever. She thanked *me* for my letter.

She told me there was a young man called Charles Drake who had studied with her in Copenhagen, and was now back in the United States. She told me about the new letter-box she planned, for training English patients as soon as she finished a book in Danish. She had been ill for some time, but she said that when she was finished with the box, she would write me again.

"You'll understand that it'll be a great happiness to me when I can help some of all my fellow-sufferers in the other lands too. I send my best wishes for your son."

Miss Norrie did not write again. She died a few months after she had written.

In the meantime, I had noted another fact that I had overlooked in the excitement of discovery. The introductory note to her article had been written by J. Roswell Gallagher, M.D., of the Adolescent Unit at Children's Medical Center, Boston. I had not taken time to question why this Dr. Gallagher had been asked to write the preface. As a matter of fact the *Bulletin* had listed only four English sources of further information on dyslexia: two were the 1896-1897 studies of Kerr and Morgan, while the third was a highly technical-sounding paper from the *Acta Psychiatry et Neurology Supplement* 1950; and there was Orton's 1937 article *Reading, Writing, and Speech Problems in Children,* so modestly entitled that after a few feeble stabs at finding it in libraries or bookshops, I gave up. There was no mention that Dr. Gallagher had written the best article to date from a parent's point of view, in the *Atlantic,* in 1948, and had published a pertinent book for laymen in 1951.

Dr. Gallagher, I discovered, was an authority on dyslexia. His experience was based on observations at Children's Center, as assistant professor of Child Health at the Harvard School of Public Health, and as school doctor at Andover, all of which provided a wealth of firsthand material.

I drafted a letter to Dr. Gallagher, retyped it neatly, addressed and stamped the envelope . . . but I never mailed it. It would be four years before Mike's path would cross Dr. Gallagher's. Now when help was available for the first time, Mike dug in his heels. He did not want any further "help," he pointed out; he had been examined, lectured to and at, prodded, helped, tutored in reading, writing, and speech; he had had his eyes and ears tested, he had been "approached" through his studies, analyzed by a "shrink," and Rorschached by what he termed "phonies." He told us that he hated his psychiatrist, and he was not sure that he trusted his father or me either. In fact, he trusted no one, and would not listen to anyone else's opinion.

His speech may have been cluttered, but he got his message through loud and clear. There were to be no more consultations, no more being yanked off to yet another expert to "find out what was wrong with him," and by God, he didn't think anything *was* wrong with him. And if there was something the matter, he insisted, then he'd outgrow it, he'd work it out for himself. If he sank, he sank.

# CHAPTER

# 8

I cannot pinpoint the moment that I realized that I must be dyslexic, that it was I who supplied the hereditary link. Certainly there was no dramatic thunderclap of recognition to match the moment when I saw that sample of Mikelike handwriting in the *Bulletin*.

In spite of what I had learned about Miss Norrie, I continued to think in terms of schoolboys. Specific language difficulties are comparatively rare among girls; outside the context of Miss Norrie's own case history I had not considered that dyslexics became adults; that the disability, although assuaged, might remain, a half-healed sore. Then, dimly I began to wonder if this could be the explanation for certain miseries of my own that had haunted me since childhood, inadequacies as mysterious as those that plagued Mike, but that I had learned to live with. What about my shyness and selfconsciousness? Had I confused cause and effect?

Out of the mists of time, came a long-suppressed unpleasant memory. It was autumn, the fall of my first year in school. I was going home from school with a group of children; with perfect clarity, I could see my red and black lunch pail. I was running ahead, calling back a phrase, mispronouncing something in such a way that I sent the group into gales of laughter. Confused, I repeated what I had said. The other children, still laughing, took up the chant, sing-songing the sentence after me, chasing me as I ran stumbling and sobbing home.

I have never been entirely at ease socially since then.

I do not pronounce words properly. In fifty years, I have learned to cover up the deficiency with a certain proficiency, a deftness. I forget words. In the middle of a sentence, the one I want will float out of my mind, the letters tumbling upward every which way like soap bubbles. My defense mechanism has been to build up a large enough vocabulary so that after a moment's hesitation I fill in with a substitute. I may have fooled the person with whom I am talking; but I experience another sting of inadequacy and frustration because I have not fooled myself. I have not said what I intended to say.

Therapists speak of the characteristic "cluttering" of dyslexic speech. My speech is definitely cluttered. I mumble, I swallow letters I am not certain of, I blur the pronunciation of a word when the soap bubbles start forming as it is half-spoken. It is a conscious device to keep people off the track.

"Speak up," said my mother, "I can't understand a thing you are saying."

"You will have to speak more clearly, Mary Louise," said

my teacher.

"Speak up," says my friend the trained singer, "get those sounds out from the bottom of your chest."

They don't know I don't *want* to speak up, that I'd rather have them think I have a speech defect than that I am so stupid I can't remember how to pronounce "syllable."

There are times when I think I am speaking clearly and then, without warning, the old familiar fogging up of the process begins. I shy away from speaking to anyone, afraid and ashamed of the way the words may come out.

I do not write in Michael's tortured script. Judging from the therapy he finally received, I can see that the old-fashioned penmanship class served something of the same purpose. We did "shaded" script with a heavy push on the downstrokes, light on the upstrokes. It gave the moment of muscular release at the bottom of the stroke that therapists depend on now. It did not teach me to spell, however, and I became as clever on my papers as I was in speech. I deliberately wrote *e* and *i*, and *o* and *a*, and smudged *n*'s and *m*'s in such a way that my teachers would be able to give me the benefit of the doubt. On the other hand, writing a short single page of a letter without mistakes remains so tiring that I do so only when the formality of the occasion demands, and I always make at least one false start.

In handwriting, for example, a combination of the loops and different heights of letters in words such as "helter" or "shelter" can be negotiated only by slowing down to kindergarten pace and writing with the carefully formed letters of a first-grader.

I have been dependent on the typewriter for years; yet I still feel compelled to append "amusing" postscripts to the effect that this is my best effort and it would do no good to

94

recopy the note since I would only make other misspellings and reversals. Obviously, someone will have corrected the spelling in this manuscript.

I do not drive. My sense of direction is too whacky; too often I point due left and say "take a right turn here," or vice versa. I cannot finish any of those I.Q. problems where arrows point in various directions. I am not sure which *is* north. After twenty years, I still cannot remember on which side of me Mike and Peter sit at dinner. Since each has had "his" side since he was old enough to sit there, this leads to hurt feelings.

There are times when *Webster's Unabridged Dictionary* does not contain the word I need to use and a substitute will not do. I realize that even the second letter of the word has eluded me. "How do you spell (mumble)?" I call in despair to my husband. He patiently stops what he is doing and asks me to define what I want to say. I do so humbly. It becomes a guessing game with him suggesting possibilities, until we hit on the one I must use. Time after time I am surprised to find how it is spelled. I thank him and proceed. It is damnably time-wasting for both of us.

Dyslexia, is going out of your way on a cold morning and being late for school because you want to avoid your mother's best friend, whose name you suddenly cannot pronounce; it is having the professor in your college writing-course sit you across from the dictionary, which you must get up and consult—to the amusement of the class—every few minutes, because he has said he will fail you for the next badly spelled paper; it is taking music lessons from the age of six, and never learning to find the notes above or below the staffs. It is working at your first job on a newspaper, a little frightened and naive, handing in your copy, and then trying to hide from the unfortunate person on the copy desk who has been given the chore of dealing with it. I recall one young man who cornered me each time, to give me an avuncular lecture on my spelling and the distress it caused him. I settled that problem quite neatly by marrying the young man, and acquiring a permanent proofreader for free.

Certainly there are far more dramatic symptoms attested to in the case histories supplied by doctors and educators. The ones I have mentioned will give you some idea of the small, everyday, hour-by-hour frustrations and embarrassments that make up the fabric of the dyslexic's existence. Trivial, small, as insignificant as the droplets of the Chinese water torture, they are ultimately as devastating.

Mike's and Miss Norrie's difficulties came to light when they were first confronted with the printed word. I had taken my first book home from the library at six, and read it. I had also begun the syndrome of not reading the letters of the individual words but seeing them in fluid patterns which made— and make—perfect sense to me. This past winter I came upon an ego-restoring explanation. In 1955, Dr. Victor H. Rosen had treated a young mathematician "a strephosymbolic," and concluded that his disturbances had resulted from "precocious reading readiness and a resultant entanglement of visual and phonetic processes" together with other conflicts that prevented the synthesis necessary to correct spelling and reading.

Experts now agree that it has always been taken for granted that children enter first grade with their auditory senses matured, and the visual lenses ready to absorb knowledge. Evidently, the auditory process is deficient in my case.

Specific language disability is hereditary. My father stammers badly. He is excellent at mathematics, but reads slowly. I have mentioned Tommy—my cousin on my father's side of the family—who also stuttered slightly. Tom not only could not be pushed through any high school, he never even learned to read.

My mother, on the other hand, had been a schoolteacher and county spelling bee champion. She had told me many times about the long lists of words she memorized the last couple of nights before each bee. (Dyslexics have fantastic short-term memories.) This past summer, as I was rummaging through an old trunk, I found some of her keepsakes: "From Micheal" she had written below one tattered drawing after another.

Mine is a mild example of specific language disability. How much of this depends on sex is impossible to establish, but not only do fewer females have the disability, they also apparently overcome it with more ease. Psychiatrists suggest that this is because the maturation process occurs earlier in female children.

I went to a small village school and high school, and a small, freshwater college. My schoolteacher mother had taught me the phonetic alphabet before first grade. On the other hand, this same system, these same teachers, were not able to teach my cousin—who was certainly as bright or brighter than I—to either read or write.

Although I had run home in tears in the first grade, by the fourth I was conscious that there were certain words such as those ending in "able" and "ible" that tripped particularly awkwardly off my tongue, so I learned to avoid them. If I had to use them I employed *aides-mémoire*. "Vegetable" was easier if I said to myself first "ve-get-able," as in "you-get-able." "Ineligible" is still beyond me, whether spoken or written.

The dyslexic eventually learns that the *aides-mémoires* themselves can betray him. For instance, for many years I remembered (and used) the spelling and pronunciation of the word for a sudden calamity, by thinking of the mildly scatological phrase "cat-ass-throw-pee." It was a shock when I discovered that what I had so proudly memorized was not quite what I thought it to be.

Directions have fared better. I may not distinguish left from right, but I can now distinguish vertical from horizontal, thanks to the book *The Grandes Horizontales;* one could be certain they were not vertical.

The soft *c* and *z* sound exactly the same to me; early on I learned to blur them into a generalized *z* sound. *T* and *ch* are heard interchangeably. This fall, for instance, I was interviewing a therapist about teaching methods. I was sitting three feet from the interviewee, facing her, when she told me I must look up the works of Sally Childs. Obediently, I wrote down "look up Sally Trials." The reason that dyslexics have so much trouble spelling correctly is becoming clear to me. I felt a fool during the Scrabble craze because I couldn't play the game. In the light of what I now know about dyslexia that is hardly surprising.

I have since analyzed the manner in which words are imprinted on my memory, and there is a definite pattern in the twists the symbols take. Words either follow this pattern, or become hopelessly jumbled. Ordinarily, I tend to speak or read the first two letters correctly. Then I skip to the third syllable, which registers either forward or backward; I come back to the second, and finish. One of the simpler examples is "lethargy" which is "legarthy" to me. It sounds right to me, and it looks right. The Rockefeller estate on the Hudson is "Potantico" Hills not "Pocantico." As far as I am concerned it is "dieturic" (diuretic), "dedragation" (degradation), and "syncophatic" (sycophantic). The tendency to twist and add a letter or syllable can be extremely frustrating. Once, it was imperative that I use the word "sacerdotal." "Saradocatal," I said to myself smugly, but I decided to look it up to make certain: it was not in the dictionary. I tried a number of possible starts, beginning with "sacra." Then I started thumbing through the "sa" words. I did learn a number of new words to be sure, but it was time consuming. I will remember the spelling for three or four days, but then it fades completely and the routine will have to be repeated.

The most damaging result of such confusions is probably psychosomatic, as it can be physically unpleasant. I have since discussed this with another dyslexic who confesses to the same symptoms: as it seems more and more impossible that one will find the word, as one becomes more and more frustrated, the sensation of a tight band being wound around the temples grows stronger and more painful. In the final stage, the dyslexic experiences definite nausea.

However, as he gets older and cares less for his public image, the dyslexic even enjoys certain small compensatory amusements. My husband and other normal people, for instance, tell me that if they want to spell "house," they can see the word, with the letters in the correct order. What I see, is the crude little box topped by triangles and chimney with smoke curling out of it that we drew in the first grade.

Listening to the news on the radio, I do not always visualize the horrors of war. When the announcer speaks of "guerrillas"—a word I must look up to be sure of the order of the u and e—I see small King Kongs, capering beneath fake palm trees. Similarly, as the war progressed, and the news became more unbearable, I read and spelled the word "Vietnam," "vitamin".

The headlines in newspapers afford a special kind of amusement too. It appears that there is a lag or overlapping in the signals from the central nervous system, so that one signal remains imprinted over a second, like a double exposure on camera film. For example, after reading about a wedding on the society page, I leafed through the amusement pages: "Peter Fonda and James Taylor Elope," I read. Hm-m! I thought. Isn't that a little far out? The headline actually read "Peter Fonda and James Taylor Flop."

By this same process of transubstantiation, "Flemming Aids Aged" becomes "Flamingo Aids Aged," "Wire Service Rejects Contract" reads "Wife Service," and "Nixon Rails at Health," not "Heath." I also have a note to myself for this chapter that speaks for itself. "Put in: 'Tettlebaum's Window/Widow! (I read it differently each time I see the ad.) "Look up and check spelling." (Typed in at a later date): "Have checked. "Widdow is right!'"

I have spent some miserable moments because of my dyslexia. I have suffered acute embarrassment and some psychiatric damage. But I feel myself incredibly lucky that either because of my female genes or my early education, specific language disability has been no more than that: a disability.

My deepest wish is that it should be discovered and treated early among the millions of children who are suffering now, so that they may know that it is not a shameful thing. So that they will not expend precious energy covering up for a deficiency they are coerced into believing connotes retardation or laziness. Just to know that there are millions like us helps reduce the strain, and the sense of being alone against the normal world.

And now, having established our knowledge of Mike's disorder, and traced the hereditary link, we shall return to that central theme of his trials and tribulations and the documentation of his progress.

# CHAPTER

# 9

As predicted, Harvard was a disaster. Or as Mike now says: "Thank God, I got my education before I went to Harvard." (Grin) "But you can't beat it as a place to tell people you went to."

The college cannot be faulted completely. Mike had been warned personally; and all freshmen are cautioned in a printed handout not to expect too much during the first two years, but the myths persist. Boys go to Harvard expecting to find heaven knows what miracles of erudition and inspired learning at the feet of the high priests of the academic world. They get pretty much the same treatment they would get at all larger colleges. They are taught mainly by graduate students, wrapped up in their own studies and the pursuit of their own degrees, while the sages themselves spend their time advising Washington, and teaching in graduate school. Harvard does indeed have a superb graduate school. The trick is to get through the undergraduate college first.

If Mike had allowed the misgivings of others to influence him, he concealed it well. He spent his weekends at Smith and Wellesley going along with the current credo that dating Cliffies was one way to end up with an inferiority complex; they were too smart.

We would ask him about his grades, but he bridled at the questions. "No sweat," he would say. It would have been sheer folly on our part to pursue the matter, for if we showed a lack of faith we could push him into failure, and we very much wanted his teachers from Groton, the doctors, and ourselves, to be proved wrong. We will never know what might have happened if he had consulted either Dr. Drake or Dr. Gallagher at that point, as Miss Norrie suggested. I believe the subsequent disaster might still have been avoided, in spite of the Groton headmaster's gloomy premonitions. But Mike remained adamant. When an appointment was set up with Dr. Drake, Mike did not show up for it. He also stopped seeing his Boston psychiatrist. When this happened, his father drove to Boston to talk the matter over with the doctor, and the latter was refreshingly candid. He agreed that Mike could not be helped by seeing him . . . "He just doesn't tell me anything no matter how I try to approach him. I have no more to go on than I did that first afternoon." We did think he might have mentioned this several months and several hundred dollars earlier.

That year was like the eye of the hurricane: the short, respite as the eye passes overhead, when the hundred-mile-per-hour winds suddenly die and the black sky is a clear blue. Then the storm starts with renewed fury. All was quiet at Harvard—too quiet. There was "no sweat," but when Mike's grades came out he had one A only, in physical training. He had not passed Freshman English, a course all Freshmen were required to take without credit because it was assumed everyone would pass it with ease. However, should anyone fail, the course had to be repeated and if it was failed again, it was taken again, and so on. A student cannot graduate without it. Mike made the passing grade in his senior year.

Dr. Schmidt and his father hoped he was adjusting; Dr. Crocker was delighted that he'd gotten through the year at all. As for Mike himself, he shrugged and didn't say anything.

That summer saw Mike in full—if not conscious—revolt. He kept the seething rebellion locked up within himself. We had no clues to his behavior until a year later. He had tried to tell us that he was sick to death of his speech and writing problems, sick of struggling against this vague disorder that made him different and filled his life with difficulties and frustrations. Whatever it was, it had forced him to work unremittingly to scrape through subjects that others found a cinch. Why couldn't he be like everyone else? Why couldn't he be like the new boy he had just met?

Meeting your Huckleberry Finn at twelve may be magical; when you're close to nineteen it can be disastrous. Mike's Huck Finn was everything Mike was not. Happy-go-lucky, irresponsible Jake had been dropped by four schools, and he carried it off as if he had been awarded a Phi Beta Kappa key. He had a flamboyant charm, a picaresque approach to life, with everything coming easy in a world that scorned middle class standards. Mike devoted all his energies that summer to trying to be as much like Jake as possible.

104

When time for college came around, Mike went off, dressed—not out of a garbage pail—but in the worst that a Times Square hole-in-the-wall had to offer. By 1968 no one would have noticed; but Jake's idea of a snappy wardrobe was several years ahead of *his* time, let alone Harvard's, where a buttoned-down shirt and clean slacks were the uniform. His acolyte went off in the tightest of form-fitting black sateen pants paired with green and purple striped shirts, all guaranteed to shrink at the first washing.

Mike truly seemed to think that if he looked like Jake, the breezy insouciance would come along with it, and would somehow transform him from the serious, miserable self he had come to loathe.

The sophomore year is notoriously difficult and—sophomoric. It is a year of experimentation, and often near panic, for the best prepared and adjusted young man, who does not know what he wants to do and is afraid to admit it.

This was multiplied a hundredfold for Mike, who was fighting within himself and against himself; wanting desperately to be what he was not, while that something was not what he really wanted at all. Mike wanted to be like jaunty devil-may-care Jake, but he also wanted the academic success that would have been his—and had been before—if only he had not been born with this burden that held him back at every step as he stumbled along the pathway to learning. It was an impossible situation, even an unbearable situation, and it tore Mike apart.

He reacted by doing many foolish and reckless things. He tried driving a car with his eyes closed half on and half off the road, at heaven knows what speed. Together with some boon companions, he locked himself in a room with an assortment of alcoholic beverages, "to see what would happen." His

105

room became known as a great spot for parties. This successful social season was climaxed with an entertainment that started toward the end of the school year and went on for days, but as the partying gained in intensity, it changed in mood, and the last night before vacation ended in hysteria. Following Mike's lead, the boys broke up their own furniture, slashed their own luggage, ripped up and ruined their clothes, and smashed bottles and crockery. After the fact, it is easy to see it as a deeply felt act of despair, a fusion of the dim realization of an ending of the way things had been, and terror of the future.

If the party climaxed the Cambridge social season, Mike's grades supplied his personal anticlimax. He had flunked out of Harvard. He was a year behind the predicted schedule, but he was out anyway. Worst of all was the E (not for excellence, but failure) in physics.

In spite of his problems and his refusal to do anything about them, his superficial dedication to the pursuit of the lighter side of college activities all year, Mike's first reaction was one of complete disbelief. He was dazed. After a few days he retreated back into his old shell.

In pushing Mike out into the world, Harvard did not make banishment absolute. The college was convinced that a boy with Mike's previous record should have performed better. Go out into the real world, he was told, get a job totally removed and dissociated from the sheltered life of a college, prove your worth at that job, and bring back a letter testifying to same at the end of the year. Then, they assured him, he would be considered for possible readmission.

Mike started pounding pavements looking for a job. He soon found that his fine education had fitted him for nothing but a menial one. He tried the agencies, but it was the same story. Messenger, stock boy, office boy: these were the only openings they had for him. Mike held out for another week before he gratefully took a job as copy boy, clerk, and general devil of all chores with a small advertising agency.

It was a more relaxed life and Mike claimed he was not missing getting an education at all. He hinted that maybe he'd skip the whole deal and be a printer, or go into advertising, or even write.

Poor Mike. The problems that had plagued his school life followed him into the business world. One day in October, the young woman who was his boss suggested that they have lunch together. She told him that he was in bad trouble, and so was she, because of him. His handwriting was so illegible that everyone was complaining. She *had* spoken to him several times about the way he kept his ad schedules and his copy list, had she not?

Mike nodded glumly. He tried to tell her that everyone had been saying the same thing since a crayon had first been put in his hand. Somehow, he had thought it would be different out of school.

School was one thing, the young woman told him, but this was the real thing, this was life. As a result of his sloppiness a serious error had resulted: *it had cost money.* As head of the department, she herself had had to shoulder the blame, and she could not let it happen again. Possibly he could afford to lose his job, she added, but she could not. Either he took the time and trouble to write legibly, or she would have no choice but to fire him.

Mike came home that night, crushed. For the first time since he had considered ditching college to advance in the world of business, he realized what would happen to him in any field he chose. He was faced with the thought that he

Before

Examples of Michael's handwriting at the beginning of his training in the Johnson Handwriting Program and after three visits.

After

REPORT FOR ........ **Michael** ........

SCHOOL ........ **Harvard** ........

**Test Sheet #1** is a sample of writing taken at the start of the program. This is a difficult passage which contains all the capitals, lower case letters and numerals.

It was written for 3 minutes.

**Test Sheet #5** is a sample taken at the end of the program.

REMARKS:

Michael came to Peterborough March 21st for a three hour consultation and interview. He has all the characteristics of the language disability dyslexic. Apparently there was some special work done with Michael at the Collegiate School at a third or fourth grade level. The fact that at Groton he had difficulty with foreign languages further indicates the pattern. His ability to excel in mathematics and sciences follows the same trend. His non-dominance of both gross motor skills and small muscle skills whereby he eats with one hand and throws a ball with another. In showing how he swung a golf club, he was not sure whether he was swinging left or right. On request he was unable to spell the word "delicate" or "indigent" because, I am quite certain, that he did not hear the words distinctly.

The original test sheet shows Michael's writing at a higher level than many of his tests and notes. Nonetheless, it is difficult going indeed. Hundred percent illegibility is an extremely rare situation. Once one learns Michael's code then the handwriting becomes readable. He writes as he is scanning the material, so that much of the writing is done neuromuscularly without his eyes seeing it. Along with this tumultuous headlong speed is the clipping and abbreviating of letter formations. On the third line I have indicated what the "h" looks like as shown in the word "there". The "h" is crossed because of the preceding "t". The body of the letter consists of a loop and in other "h's" throughout the passage even this loop is eliminated. To attempt to slow down a writer and to rebuild deteriorated symbols at this age would be an incredibly difficult task.

The report written by Mr. Johnson on completion of the program.

109

might never get a chance to choose, but that his life would be a succession of illpaid, boring jobs, from which he would be fired anyway because of that quirky malevolence that would not let him do what he knew he could do.

It was a Friday night, and Mike played his bongo drums long and desperately. He had estranged himself from us for so long that I lay in my room in the dark, not daring to get up and ask him to tell me about it. Next morning, Mike asked abruptly for the names of the people whom Miss Norrie had recommended. On his own, he obtained names of people near to New York and his job, and began his sessions with Dr. Schmidt again. He could talk to her, he trusted her as he did no one else, and she comforted him and alleviated the emotional strain that was building up so dangerously.

He got in touch with Warren T. Johnson, the best-known handwriting therapist, who now—frail and in his seventies—had retired to Peterborough, New Hampshire. Mike typed out a letter to him, explaining his difficulties and asking if he might come and see him. Mr. Johnson replied that since he had retired, he was no longer giving help to individuals. Mike tried again, this time making his request in a handwritten note. Back came a quick reply. Now Mr. Johnson would see him. "It is very seldom that I have encountered handwriting which is almost completely indecipherable," he explained.

Mike only went to New Hampshire a few times, but the results were magical. After the very first session, although he was not writing well, he was writing clearly. Mr. Johnson wrote out a complete diagnosis of his troubles, explaining scientifically what the dyslexic must overcome, and giving Mike scores of little tricks and short cuts that would relax the muscles of his fingers and wrist and get him through an ordinary paper.

He did not promise an always legible handwriting at this late date in Mike's development, and he suggested that Mike type out lengthy material, and type also whenever undue stress might cause his muscles to tense uncontrollably. Most important of all, he gave Mike the encouragement to believe that he could write legibly for short periods of time.

Armed with this new hope, and Dr. Schmidt's assurances, Mike went to his department head and asked her to give him time to work at his handwriting and type everything possible. Would she recheck his lists and duties, and stand behind him he asked? People seem to like Mike, and she agreed to do so for a month, but not one day more. She meant it, and Mike knew that she did.

The office janitor, who did not even aspire to the lowly job of copy boy, provided Mike with more food for thought during this month. He was a very nice young man, and Mike could not understand his passivity, his way of taking for granted that this was all the world would ever give him. They started talking over their sandwiches. Mike discovered that the boy had quit school in the ninth grade, completely discouraged. He could not read and could barely write, and had been passed along from teacher to teacher until they were glad to get rid of him. Now, he was running around at night with young toughs and other dropouts and getting in trouble himself, mainly because he could not make enough money to hang out with the fellows he would have liked to have been with.

"I think Jerry has the same thing I have—dyslexia—" Mike told me, "only no one has ever bothered to do anything about it."

After this, he became his old silent self and the boom of the bongo drums resounded more menacingly than before. One

111

night while my husband was on a trip, instead of shutting himself up in his room, Mike came into mine at about eleven o'clock, and plopped himself down on my chaise. I was already in bed, propped up on pillows, and ready to read myself to sleep. Mike had not followed me into my room except for money since the time of his childhood nightmares. At first, he seemed to have nothing world-shattering on his mind, a play he wanted to see . . . did I think he could afford a second-hand car in the spring out of his earnings? There was a tooth he thought should be looked after. . . .

Abruptly, he turned the talk to his future. Did he have one he wondered? He was writing more legibly now, but he knew how much the effort cost him in concentration that he should be free to give to work itself. He was certain he would never spell. In spite of his troubles he could grasp the sense of what he was reading, even though he still had trouble speaking specific sentences. The writing should be less of a problem after he finished college, because he would use his typewriter. Did I think it possible, he wondered, that his teachers would let him use it now, maybe even for the examinations?

Yes, he had decided he would go back to school. He was no more fitted for the business world than the scholastic one, and he would need all the education he could get. He wanted to go back to Harvard, too, if they would take him. He knew we would disapprove, but he explained that it was a challenge, an ego-thing. They had kicked him out, and he was going to prove that he could get back in, and stay. He would rather settle for all C's there than take some gut courses and whiz by in the top third of the class in some second-rate college.

I made little comment, for this was a rambling monologue, as if Mike were talking to himself. He went on to say that Dr. Schmidt was making him understand himself and lots of other things better. He delved deeper and deeper into his

112

childhood memories, not absolutely sure of what he really remembered and what he might have reconstructed from hearing us talk.

As suddenly as he had switched from trivia to consideration of his future, Mike began talking about his past, almost unintelligible in his intensity. He gave me his own version of that "perfect summer." Not once had anyone let him know that his babblings had not been understood. Mike was talking, he said, speaking as clearly as every single one of those silly, smiling ladies, who had laughed and made fun of him. As he went from beach umbrella to beach umbrella, he knew that he was being humored, that his factual remarks were not being answered correctly, that he was being indulged or brushed aside at whim. He would wait for answers to his questions, and then, in a whirlwind of frustration, run down the beach away from a puzzle that was too much for him.

He had always believed that the grownups were playing a particularly sadistic game. Since he spoke precisely as they sounded to him, he felt they could not fail to understand. Yet, for some mysterious reason they seemed to have chosen to mock him, pretending that they did not.

It was not until this winter, he said, starting with his problems at work and hearing Jerry tell his story, that he had begun to wonder whether he was right, or whether there might not be another side to the story. . . . His voice trailed off.

I looked at that six feet of mute appeal, waiting for my verdict, and found it difficult to speak. How could I convey the horror of what he had told me? How could I make him understand that he had been the beach baby, the positively adored pet of all those adults, none of whom would have hurt him in the slightest way for a second? I tried to tell him, but I was not sure if he truly believed me.

From then on we went step by step through his "loving, protected childhood."

Given his original premise—that adults had first amused themselves with his speech, and had refused to understand him for reasons known only to themselves, and had continued to deliberately misunderstand him as he grew older—it was a miracle that Mike had survived emotionally until now. No wonder that he had finally broken down at fifteen.

He had hated museums, but he *had* loved riding the buses and the El's despite the fact that I did everything I could to spoil the excursions by telling him to look at this and not miss that, when he was having a splendid fantasy about being the driver. He liked the motion up there at the front of the bus, the scary sense that he might bump into something. He did not want to know where he had been, or where he was going, or what landmarks he was passing.

He did not see much difference between the television he was allowed to watch only on Saturday mornings and "the stimulating experience of growing up in a literate family." He couldn't tune out the dinner conversations, or switch channels—all that talk about words, and meanings, and quotations. As far as Mike was concerned, we might just as well have been having an old-fashioned family quarrel about the rent, or who spent how much for what.

He had hated my chasing him around the apartment in an attempt to help with his homework. It was just another example of unreasonable adult tyranny he pointed out.

At last I spoke up. I explained what a miserable time I had had in high school and college, always being trotted out in front of the class to look up some word. I truly was trying to help him over what I hoped was some temporary aberration

114

so that he would be spared the same embarrassment. I reminded him that at the time I hadn't known what his troubles were. Mike considered for a minute.

"You mean that when you'd tell me to look up a word for myself and then look it up yourself afterward you weren't trying to put me down?" he asked.

Why had I never told him I couldn't spell much better than he? Possibly I had been ashamed to, or thought it might make his troubles worse. At the time, I was as confused as he. We agreed—now that it was too late—that as misery loves company, it might have been smarter on my part to have said, "let's look up this word together," instead of sneaking off on my own a couple of minutes later to make sure how it was spelled.

My six-footer eyed me quizzically. "Jees, Louise," he said, deliberately employing one of my less favorite salutations, "you panicked."

"Yep," I agreed, "I panicked."

Since then, when I charge off to the dictionary, Mike glances after me with a half-pitying, half-conspiratorial, we-belong-to-the-same-secret-society look.

The conversation had gone on for six hours, but I could sense there was still something on his mind. He was hedging, but I was beginning to guess what he wanted to say. The insouciance he had shown after he had been bounced from college was totally false. He had been shattered. He was still not over it. He rambled on, stopped, and started again. Why had he taken those foolish chances he mused? Had he driven so recklessly out of some deep-seated self-destructive urge? That final party at Harvard had been an equally overt manifestation of the symptom. Mike had come dangerously close to the end of his rope.

I recalled that Mike had been paying for his sessions with Dr. Schmidt this year he took off from Harvard. It is a device approved by the majority of psychologists to help the patient understand the importance of making use of the time spent in therapy. Dr. Schmidt soon called me and asked that we not allow it in Mike's case. Even now, he felt this as a further rejection, and instead of helping, it was harming his progress.

Now, with the help of his "teacher" and other good advisers, and with the strength of his own stubborn character to back him up he began fighting his way back. There would be bad days ahead, bad weeks, and discouragements but things would never be as bad again as they had been in that winter, that season of despair when Mike had almost succumbed to the despair.

Mike got his letter from his employer, and was accepted back at Harvard. He jogged along with C's and a B or so— mostly because the grades now were determined by term papers—and the professors could read what he had typed. Then came another academic blow. Advanced biology was his favorite course, and he had read much outside material, staying extra time in the laboratory on his own, and doing well in his experiments. He felt confident that he knew as much on his subject as anyone in the class, and was looking forward to a B at the least, although he expected an A. The written examination was to take three hours, but Mike was certain that a biology professor would understand his problem and permit him to type his exam in an empty room next door.

The professor did not understand. On the contrary, he had never heard of dyslexia. He did not believe there was such a thing and implied Mike was planning to cheat. He was adamant: Mike would write his paper by hand, in the examina-

116

tion room, with everyone else.

The reader has only to turn back to Miss Norrie's description of the dyslexic under strain, to know what happened. Tension fed on tension until Mike could barely hold a pen. But he did know his subject, and somehow he filled three blue books. They were returned unread, a big E scrawled across the front. "I have not injured my eyes trying to discover what you are attempting to say." Mike's messiness and carelessness, the note continued, were beyond the professor's comprehension. The final, damning verdict read, "Clarke should not aspire to a career in anything so exacting as the sciences." All the same, he passed with a D.

Fortunately, the arrogance made Mike mad. His common sense prevailed; he was growing up, and the professor might be unpleasant, but he was a superlative teacher. Mike had learned a lot, more than he might have learned elsewhere. His lab work had to be good to make up for that E. Better a good teacher and a barely passing grade, he thought, than the other way around.

The hell with grades from now on, he decided. He was going to take only courses that interested him, squeaking by to graduate. Chemistry, of course, but also Chinese literature, and a course centering around his favorite Beethoven quartets.

"But you can't read music," I protested.

"Oh, you don't need to," Mike assured me airily. "It's the cerebration behind them."

Mike was soon disabused of this quaint notion; it had never occurred to the professor that anyone who could not read music would sign up. So we devised an instant sightreading course for dyslexics. In spite of the fact that he could not carry a tune, Mike had a good ear for music and his mathematical aptitude worked in his favor. We approached the subject through his aural, visual and tactile senses. We began by throwing out the classic progression from C natural scale through first the sharps, and then the flats. Mike could hear the C major chord. He could hear what happened when it was changed to the dominant seventh chord; he could hear the logical progression from that dominant seventh into F major. So we chased majors and dominants through the last of the flats, and then, backward from six sharps down through one sharp, finishing with C natural again.

Mike's logical mind at once accepted and enjoyed the certainty, the indestructibility of the scale patterns, where a definite combination of whole notes and half notes would always be the same, whether starting on C natural or G flat. We pounded them out together. Mike copied the scales and chords and signatures into one of those notebooks with the wide staffs they give to primary children. I made a tape for him to take back to Cambridge for future reference. Mike did not learn to play the piano, but he could follow the scores of the Quartets. And he got a C in the course.

In October of his senior year, Mike had told me that he would like to talk with Dr. J. Roswell Gallagher, the expert he had refused to allow me to contact nearly five years before.

Dr. Gallagher answered almost immediately. Because of previous commitments, he could not see Mike on any regular basis. But he would, however, talk with his friend, Dr. Graham B. Blaine, Jr. "Dr. Blaine is a psychiatrist, and I'll explain to your son that he does not need a psychiatrist, but Dr. Blaine is at Harvard and I do think it would be helpful for [there to be] somebody on hand in a position to help him work this thing out."

118

He concluded, "One of my young friends whose handwriting is no doubt equally impossible, did graduate from Harvard. I used to dread receiving notes from him: I just plain couldn't read them, but at least I always knew who they were from!"

Dr. Gallagher did manage to see Mike several times during the year. Possibly nothing in his life until then was as important to him as those sessions. Dr. Gallagher, of course, was tops in his field. He also combined great understanding of Mike's disability with a skill for interpreting the thoughts of boys born of a lifetime of listening to boys. He talked with Mike in a way no one had ever done before. No psychiatrist could have counseled him better. In that brief year, under the doctor's aegis, Mike was able to put together the pieces of the puzzle that was his life.

Another interested mentor entered the picture during that year. Daniel H. Funkenstein, M.D., of the Harvard Medical School, examined Mike, talked with him, and began giving him more good advice to help him on his way. In the last few weeks of his final semester at Cambridge, Mike talked for the first time with the master of his house, Dr. John Finley. Doctors Gallagher, Funkenstein, and Finley between them penetrated the last line of his defenses.

Mike did not see Chinese literature and dabbling in music as an end in themselves. He would be unhappy as long as he was denied that "exacting career in the sciences" that his biology professor considered so unrealistic for him. The career he sought demanded years at medical school. With his miserable grades and with no recommendations from the head of his department he was as badly off in his way as Jerry the janitor.

Dr. Finley did some research into Mike's records. Mike had

achieved B's in Harvard's toughest chemistry courses; he had persevered. He talked with the people at Mike's old school and he got in touch with Dr. Gallagher.

At graduation Mike was lost in the throng of also-squeaked-bys, in the lowest fifth of the class. The diplomas are distributed after the formal ceremony, at a luncheon for parents and boys in the various houses. The cum laudes and athletes are easy. But at least each boy gets called by name, and the hard-pressed master finds something to say about each. As Mike walked forward, Dr. Finley announced: "Mike is going to take special courses in his chosen field after graduation as preparation for medical school." I think it was as much of a surprise to Mike as it was to us. He was going to get his chance. The short vacation he had planned before looking for a job was scrapped. Instead, on the Monday after the Saturday of commencement day, encouraged by Dr. Finley, and with Dr. Gallagher's support, Mike was looking—not for just a job—but for one which would be a step toward medical school and the career he had always dreamed of.

# CHAPTER

# 10

Encouraging Mike did not include finding the job for him. That was to be a part of proving he had the determination and character to back up his ambitions. His apprenticeship might take one, but would probably take two years.

Once again, luck took a hand in his destiny. Mike appeared at the employment office of a large teaching laboratory. He was sent, routinely, to the department that would complete his salvation. Another friend of Mike's, with identical aspirations but different problems, applied at the laboratory the next day. He was shuffled off to another department, a boring dead-end sort of place, where he could have stayed for years without advancing his learning. Discouraged, he gave up before the winter was over. He has made a commendable niche for himself as a high school teacher, but he is not doing what he had hoped to do, and he has not forgotten it.

Mike's job was prettied up with the title of lab assistant, but his duties consisted mostly in washing test tubes, mopping up, and cleaning out the cages of animals used in the experiments. It was menial enough that the employment office had not asked for any qualifications, or inquired about Mike's education. Even so, he found the work engrossing. Since no one told him not to, he took to hanging around after his day's stint was over. Some six weeks after he started, Mike was in the background when a minor contretemps occurred, and he was the person to hand over the instrument the doctor had called for.

Recalling the incident, the doctor was surprised that Mike would know what he had wanted, and told him to drop by and see him. He asked where Mike had gone to school, and what he had studied; it was an easy step for Mike to tell him what he hoped to accomplish after he had worked in the laboratory. This was Mike's first experience with the advantages of saying where he had gone to college. "Harvard! What in the world are you doing here?" Without informing Mike, the head of the department sent off to Harvard for his records.

Meanwhile, he had not been forgotten at Harvard. In July came a short note from Dr. Funkenstein—"you must go to Columbia at night in the fall and study physical chemistry." —Dr. Funkenstein took it for granted that Mike was going to succeed. By the time the records arrived, Mike had been working in the lab for some four months, being given more and more small, but privileged tasks to perform. The laboratory had a computer that delighted him. Here was a logical machine he could easily understand, and learn to run. He

122

made himself available to keep track of data on experiments where the researchers were unable or too busy to do the chore themselves.

On the afternoon that Mike was called into the head office, he faced a very puzzled scientist. After that first encounter, the members of the department had been interested in Mike's potential. They had been baffled by the fact that Mike had graduated from Harvard. Now, after observing his work for three more months they were thoroughly confused when the grades came.

"How could a guy as bright as you have gotten such lousy grades?" asked the doctor.

"Easy," Mike said, and once more poured out his life history. Mike's case aroused the further interest of the department. Some had not heard of dyslexia; two knew doctors who had completed their training despite this disability. More letters were written: Dr. Finley confirmed the character and potential, Dr. Gallagher added his word, and confirmed the diagnosis.

That winter was not easy but it was immensely satisfying. Mike cleaned out his cages where the cats for experiments were kept, and mopped up, but he began to help with the preparation for the experiments, and was allowed to keep charts, and to observe. He was given one small experiment to perform himself, and write up the results. He took to going to the laboratory on his days off to look in on his own experiment and whatever other ones he was keeping track of. Usually he worked a ten-hour day. He sent progress reports to Dr. Gallagher, Dr. Funkenstein and Dr. Finley.

"His" department agreed with Dr. Funkenstein and he enrolled at Columbia to take additional science courses at night. The laboratory head was now prepared to help all he could, but realistically, Mike would have to have something more to offer than the Harvard grades and the year's experience in the lab. He would have to produce an A in Physical Chemistry before the department could honestly forward its recommendation to a medical school. Mike hadn't had an A since he left Groton.

There was nothing to do but plug away and hope. As the winter progressed, Mike was called in again and told—cautiously—that he might try getting letters out to the schools; it was very late for the next year, but he might get on the advance list for the following year and if that A came through someone might have a place not already filled.

Mike set about composing his letters. He was determined that they would start with his grades from Harvard, and the history of his language difficulties.

"If I were the admissions officer and I found all that tacked on at the end, I'd chuck the application in the wastebasket," he reasoned. Better to be chucked out at once rather than waste good will for a second try, which he must make if his first balloons were shot down.

In all, Mike mailed thirty-six letters. All but three were answered. Half had already filled their quotas, as anticipated. Ten suggested that—if he were not accepted elsewhere—they would be happy to put him on their list for the following year. One of these was Harvard Medical School.

Of course, he was turned down cold by several schools, but eight took the trouble to write to his department head, and four were interested enough to set up interviews.

There was one revealing incident. Mike was turned down because of the dyslexia, by the school his department had felt certain would take him. He showed the letter to one of the doctors with whom he was working.

124

"Why that's from old So-and-so!" The doctor burst out indignantly, "I happen to know he is dyslexic himself!"

Mike completed his modest experiment and wrote his paper. The head's faith was rewarded; he got his A in Physical Chemistry, and flew out for an interview at the school where he had hoped he might go. It was too good to be true, he told us when he came back. The doctors were wonderful, the program was better than he had heard and the equipment was superb. They assured Mike that his dyslexia would not be a factor in their decision.

We sat down to wait it out. In the meantime, he was accepted by a second school. This one even noted that it was particularly interested in what a dyslexic might accomplish. Three weeks went by, and the suspense grew. The second school did not offer precisely what Mike wanted, but dared he be choosy? Ten months before he would not have believed he could achieve this much.

At the last possible moment the Marines rode up. The postman brought the letter of acceptance from the school Mike wanted—but it contained an "if,"—Mike would be accepted on the condition that he passed in the top half of his class in the first year.

Mike decided to take the gamble. His life had accustomed him to conditions.

Mike's golden sunrise came in February, with winds howling and snow pelting down from gray skies. A letter arrived from the Committee of the Faculty: Mike had done well during the first semester; he was in the top ten in his class of one hundred. The condition had been removed, and Michael Clarke was now a student in full standing.

# CHAPTER

# 11

As this book neared completion, it seemed only fair to let Mike tell his story in his own words, explain his feelings, give an assessment of his disability and how it had affected him. He recorded the following on tape before reading anything I had written, since we agreed he should give his evaluations uninfluenced by others. The reader will note that his recollections differ at times from the previous chapters. In fact, since it was a stream-of-consciousness talk, with as little direction as possible, there are times when his own memories at different ages reflect different reactions to a given episode.

Q. We talked about your preschool life quite a while ago. Do you remember much about school itself?

A. The first four grades were the worst. The whole fourth grade has just blacked out, it was so bad. In the third and fourth grades I always did the problems right but I'd put down the wrong answers and the teachers would make me do them over and over again. I kept making the same mistakes that way, of course. The teachers wouldn't help me or tell me what was wrong, and kept telling me to find out for myself.

The kids picked on me until after the fourth grade. I felt short, and inadequate, although looking back, I wasn't the smallest, really. They made fun of me and kicked at me, that sort of undercover stuff you couldn't really complain about. Mr. Klein was just as bad—funny, he's the only one whose name I can remember. He was one of those gone-to-fat athletes, very gung-ho. A nasty man.

The third grade teacher made me read out loud all the time. Phonics? I don't remember anything special. Just having to read out loud and I couldn't. It was torture, of course, and no one understood me.

No, as I said, I can't remember any of their names until I got to fifth grade. The teacher there got me doing math, as opposed to just numbers. Sixth grade made the big change— algebra and Latin—especially Latin. It was logical. For the first time I was reading something, and spelling the words, too. I don't understand yet what made the difference. Was it because I was always reproducing specific symbols, generating my own data?

It's funny, I can remember almost everything about Mr. Strange, Mr. Fry, Mr. Westgate and Mrs. Leistikow at Saint Bernard's, while those others at Collegiate are all blocked out. Sometimes I think maybe I *had* to do well after having them. They were really great teachers. I mean, maybe I could have done without any more formal schooling. I know it's silly but

127

I have thought of it.

Anyway, that was the first time I'd been at the top of the class, in math and Latin. I think it made a big difference psychologically. Curiously enough, I think it affected the teachers' attitudes toward me just as much—it made them more concerned—or maybe it was simply a reciprocity process. When I did well they got more interested, and when they got concerned, I did better.

The pattern was repeated all through Groton. I realize now that I got one hell of an education, the very best. I didn't, then. I don't mean I thought it wasn't good, I just never thought about it at all . . . I took it for granted. I don't think I really understood how good it all was until I got into Med School.

As for Harvard . . . the first year is awfully fuzzy. It was quite a big change, though I didn't know how much at the time. I was awfully young for my age or something. But that second year . . . (long pause, then a spate of words). You know, I never studied so hard in my life. I worked harder than I ever had before—or since, for that matter—that's what made it so shattering. I wasn't a bit prepared for what happened. I was sure I was in the top of the class—I really *knew* everything. And then I got nothing but D's and that F. I would have had two, if I hadn't dropped Chem. 20. And then I went back and got a B.

The year off helped. Maybe everyone should take a year off, no matter if they're having trouble or not. It changed a lot of my attitudes and I wouldn't have looked so bad, if that sonofabitch hadn't thrown out my final paper in Biology. I just felt better about what I was doing, and yet wasn't working nearly as hard as the first two years. It was more like being back in Groton.

Of course, Dr. Schmidt and Dr. Gallagher made a lot of difference in those two years. Dr. Schmidt would make me recall specific incidents from childhood and relate them to my present problems. It was therapy, but now I think of it more as an exercise in recall, in trying to convey specific images. It helped to clarify my memory, and especially to organize the images. She had that gift of being able to make me feel so strongly that *I* was helping *her*. That meant a lot, beyond the actual process of putting the things together.

I'd say the typewriter was the device that helped me most. You get bored and tired, writing by hand. Your hand is so much slower than your thoughts. With a typewriter, your hands know where a bunch of letters is on the keyboard, and your hand rolls in the proper direction. It helps, too, by giving you a concrete letter. I think they should teach all dyslexic kids with typewriters, so that they can have a permanent record of what they see on a page.

When I look back—when it comes to images—I realize I have to reconstruct them from bits and pieces. There is a lack of ability in my mind's eye to reconstruct whole scenes. I have to vocalize them and try to put them together, because the whole I have is a vague, murky type of thing, without much color.

I have thought the trouble might lie in two areas. One might be that the actual primary imprint as received by the central nervous system was weak after the visual image had been received by the eye, so that when it traveled down the nerves of the eye to the brain it somehow didn't register very strongly. So that when registrations to the brain were categorized and put in associational areas for retrieval, the primary image was not strong enough. The brain could not distinguish this input from other images and so put the image in a unique associational area. When the time came to retrieve it, it might not be located in this unique spot and an associated image was retrieved instead.

The other possibility is that the primary image may have been okay but there was some fault with the association in the brain. I believe this to be less likely, since if it were true, the person would have a number of similar difficulties, in reasoning, for example. Dyslexia does not affect my reasoning.

When one tries to analyze how one handles oneself it is hard to say that a specific series of events or a single event led to this or that. For instance, a lot of things happened during that year off, and Dr. Schmidt was one of them. In my senior year at college, a lot of things occurred, and Dr. Gallagher was one of them.

Dr. Schmidt certainly strengthened my memory, as I mentioned a minute ago. As my hypothesis suggested, if one has weak images, practice in talking about them teaches one to extract the most information from them. I still have trouble with weak images. Before, I was only able to present them as they were, vague fragments. Now I take a couple of seconds to consider them, and try to extract the information before I go ahead and describe them. It is sort of the same thing as the television camera going past Mars and extracting information from the impulses coming out.

Dr. Gallagher was doing somewhat the same thing, only from the opposite direction. He was strengthening my input, not the retrieval area. The idea was that somehow or other you could train yourself to pay more attention to what was going on. Obviously you see *something*, but lots of people see a thing once and it is there. They don't waste time. I spend too much time seeing it over and over before I am satisfied that I really have it. The same is true of research. You have to be better organized, so you think about every action you make, and how it relates to the previous action, then you can plan ahead better.

A couple of other things occur to me, too. When a person has been struggling to get a concrete view of the world, the tendency is to stick with it. After a while, you think that any view you can come up with that seems to agree with the majority of people is the one to hold onto. Now I have learned to go the opposite way. I spend a long time taking that image I share with other people apart, and looking at it in a way different from the rest of the world. Creativity is taking ordinary images and relevant facts apart and restructuring these rather random images in an entirely new way. Picasso did it in his abstract paintings.

It is only our cultural training which says that certain colors go together, or dictates that certain lines form a cat or a bed. What happens in research is that certain ideas are culturally defined. Research says that while these may be the facts, there is no reason why one should follow their previous orientation. That is one of the big problems I had. Actually, in doing research, I discovered that all through my life until then I hadn't been willing to depart from the presented orientation. I was never strong enough to examine facts except in the light of the way a particular person presented them to me. I was just so pleased when I could retrieve the pattern of the original presentation. I think, too, that I was always afraid that if I didn't retrieve them in the original pattern I wouldn't be able to retrieve them at all. I'd lose everything.

Q. What about sports? Did they bother you after those first four grades?

A. Well, I've never been a great athlete. I wasn't much of anything at first. Probably the fact that I had fast reflexes made up for a lot of things. A really good athlete has fast reflexes, but an average guy is slower, and I could train myself. I learned to start a little sooner and give myself a margin for error. The average athlete would achieve the same result more smoothly, and faster, but we'd end up at the same time. I was in the fifth or sixth grade before I picked this up. (Grin.) Of course, I could always run fast.

(That you could.)

My hand-eye coordination was never very good and it still isn't. But I wouldn't tell dyslexics to stay away from sports, just competitive sports that put a premium on hand-eye coordination, like baseball or handball. I am still quite awkward at handball. Anything where the margin for error is small. Tennis and squash allow for a margin of error. They demand coordination, but you can get away with it; you don't have to hit the ball every time at dead center of the racquet.

Football and crew, too, put a premium on other things. You can't control your own size or strength, but speed can make up for size, and coordination is a plus. It doesn't make that much difference in grade school or high school. A fast one-hundred-and-fifty-pounder can make it against a slow one-hundred-and-seventy-five-pounder. College is different, of course.

The biggest thing at Saint Bernard's and Groton were those teams at all levels. You could always find a place to play, and it was no big deal if you didn't happen to win. Maybe you didn't know it, but that is one of the reasons I went to Groton. I wasn't so hot on the hand-eye combination, but other kids had lousy reflexes, and it all came out even, we could play on the same team.

And you can improve. You can learn, if you get the chance to practice, especially if you're not tense and overmatched.

132

That was another good thing at school. Sooner or later your brain does remember that the ball you are trying to control is coming at you and you learn to gauge it. I think you learn by practicing. Kids ought to practice playing catch even if they never play baseball. Get their father to throw the ball and not expect them to hit or make a big thing out of it.

For one thing, this past year or so, I gradually became aware that all the guys I was playing squash with were getting worse and worse. It wasn't until the last month or so that I got the idea that maybe I was getting better. And then there was that *Tippecanoe* thing. (*Tippecanoe* is a game that depends on a quick turn of a tilted bar to send a small steel ball back and forth down nine bars into a cup without letting it fall off.) I couldn't believe it when I did it before either Pop or Peter who always have been so much better coordinated than I. I would guess that I'm better coordinated now.

Q. Is there anything else you recall specifically?

A. It's hard for me to analyze the whole thing because it was all so gradual, and anyway, I was so involved with the problem myself. I don't think a person in that position really registers what is going on. I can't recall when I got into the problem and started analyzing things for myself. When you are aware of a problem, and you start trying to sort things out, it is too late for you to go back. You're standing outside yourself like everyone else. So you can't ask me to say what I think about some vague problem, or something that happened. You have to spell it out, the question would have to be specific, like "did this or that happen?" Then I could go back to the actual incident, but I need the direction; I can't recall it in a general frame of questioning.

Q. But I don't want to direct you or influence you. If your memories are just hazy, that would be a part of it being you.

A. (Mike, going on, as if talking to himself, evidently not listening . . .) I can't recall any special year, and it's no good even asking me about third grade or the summer I was thirteen or anything. That is all a part of it. It was a dark period. I have to have someone lead me through it.

Q. Were you unhappy?

A. When I was little? I don't think so. If you think everyone is the same way . . .

Q. You thought everyone was the same way?

A. Yeah. How was I to know? You take a colorblind person or a deaf person—especially deaf—they have a hard time understanding what it's like to hear. I never thought I had special problems. I supposed everyone caught balls that way, and you know about yourself, when you read the words you know what they mean and they look all right to you. Later, I just thought it was a subtle thing, a degree. I could do math and Latin, and some kids couldn't, and they could spell and talk plain, and I couldn't. How was I supposed to know?

The math, though, that could be depressing. I guess I knew something was wrong when I'd have everything worked out, and at the last minute I'd make some simple, stupid mistake. That was frustrating. Or I'd do the whole long equation right and put down the wrong answer. That's something I don't do any more, but getting confused still bothers me. Other people put down wrong answers because they don't know. I know, but some place along the line something happens, there is a reversal and I transpose figures; it's part of the retrieval thing.

I found out that when I try working things out in my head, they get flipped around a little bit. So now I've learned never to think things out. I put an awful lot of reliance on putting things down on paper that other people carry around in their heads. Maybe no one else can read it, but it's down. I don't

134

take pages and pages of notes, but I have something down for everything. Sort of direction finders. I never rely on my memory for anything.

Another thing, I still fall asleep in a class if I'm not writing, lectures seem to actually hypnotize me. I try to absorb what is being said, but it's no good. I need the activity of writing what is being said and it helps me absorb the sense of a lecture, as well as giving me the notes I was talking about.

I'd say I have to write with my hand to remember. That's what I learned most in my senior year, from Dr. Gallagher and Blaine. It's part of the physical imprinting. I think that if I never saw my notes again, I'd have a better grasp of the subject than I possibly could have gotten by just listening. And when I can't read my notes, sometimes, I can pick out the gist and key phrases.

Now, in research, I've learned never to go over a problem if it comes out wrong. I start all over again from scratch.

Q. What do you mean?

A. I rip the page right off and don't look at it again, because it will just imprint the mistake more deeply each time I go over it. I never go back; I never try to find the mistake. And I don't want to see the old solution. I might not pick up the mistake, but I have found from experience that the chances are that I will, the second time around. My reason for doing everything on paper isn't because, like some people, I think paper is the logical place to work. I use paper as my mind's eye, so to speak. I put numbers all over the place when I am working so I can see them. When I can see them, I don't have to waste all that energy, trying to hold an image.

I'd say that this seems to trigger the retrieval, which is why I don't make the mistake second time around. Of course, I don't dare make mistakes anymore. One wrong figure, and

135

I'd be out a month of work.

Actually, I don't seem to have as much trouble as I used to. Maybe it's like the squash and *Tippecanoe,* or practicing for any other game.

As Mike was finishing this tape, he passed his dissertation for his Ph.D. and drank the traditional glass of champagne. He is working toward a further degree. He hopes, someday, to make his contribution to science.

By a fortuitous chain of circumstances Mike's story became one of fulfillment. He had a family who refused to accept the verdict of the educational system, and he was given the chance to get the kind of schooling that proved effective for him. In the long run, his greatest asset was his own indomitable personality.

As I look back, happy for Mike, I still say it is wrong. Wrong that every child does not have precisely the same chances. It takes so little, and costs so little in comparison with the interest neglect collects over the years. The opportunities should be taken for granted; they should be offered eagerly instead of having to be fought for.

# CHAPTER

# 12

The statistics of diminishing returns constitute one of the most dramatic and alarming aspects of dyslexia. There is a possibility of an eighty-two percent recovery for the child if he receives proper instruction in the first grade; by the end of the third grade, this possibility is reduced to forty-three percent. Thus, to the dyslexic child and his parents, the educators' wait-see practice of delaying testing until the third grade is a greater threat than the "look-say" method of teaching reading.

Today's parents have a formidable weapon—a system of reliable warning signals—which was not available until the mid-sixties. Studies and evaluations had been going on long before this time, but until the results were published, there was no way for the general public to be aware of what testing had been done and, most important, drawn.

Doctors and educators who cared, and there were precious few who did, could refer to neurologist Dr. Samuel T. Orton's 1933 description of the classic dyslexic preschool child: he noted that parents invariably reported that these children had been gay and exceptionally healthy, until faced with the necessity of mastering the skills of reading and writing in school. It was Orton who noted that one symptom was invariably present: strephosymbolia, the twisting of symbols.

By 1961 results of other studies were becoming available. However, they were written for the expert, with few concessions to the layman. Archie A. Silver, M.D., and Rosa A. Hagin, Ph.D., published the results of their studies with children at Bellevue Hospital in an article entitled "Diagnostic Considerations in Children with Reading Disability" in the Bulletin of the Orton Society. In 1964, the New York Infirmary summarized the work it had done for fifteen years in its Reading Clinic under the direction of the late Fannie S. Mendelsohn in a privately published paper entitled "The Treatment of Reading Disability." Katrina de Hirsch and Dr. Jeannette Jansky made public their studies at the Pediatric Language Disorder Clinic, at Columbia Presbyterian Medical Center in New York City, in "Psychological Correlates of the Reading Process" in the International Reading Association Proceedings, 1962.

However, material remained so sparse that as late as 1966, Dr. Malcolm Critchley, President of the World Federation of Neurologists and Chairman of the Research Group on Developmental Dyslexia suggested that, above all, the experts needed a comprehensive study of dyslexics from birth through childhood and into early middle age. "Too many times we see them (dyslexics) as children and then they are lost clinically, or they do not come to us at all until they are adults." Mike's life story can supply this continuity; his personal comments should be useful to researchers as well as parents.

Today, a parent can consult some ten or twelve sources and put together a list of signs that seem to indicate the presence of dyslexia, but in order to do so he would need more than a passing acquaintance with scientific terminology. The symptoms listed below constitute the most complete list of the physical, psychological, ophthalmological, and auditory manifestations of dyslexia that has been published to date. They have been culled from the sources listed in the bibliography of this book, as well as privately published papers delivered at various medical conferences by Katrina de Hirsch, Dr. Leon Eisenberg, Roger E. Sanders, and Dr. Herman Krieger Goldberg. A number of them may sound rather far-fetched; the author can only remind the reader that fifty years ago the educated world laughed at the peasants who believed they could cure sores by binding them with mouldy bread—until Dr. Fleming came along.

However, Dr. John Money of Johns Hopkins warns that "just as in physical diseases, there is not one symptom you can pounce on and say triumphantly this is (or is not) a proof of dyslexia . . . out of context, each sign might be encountered in the healthy."

## FAMILY HISTORY/HEREDITY

The first indication of a congenital tendency toward dyslexia will be found in a family that includes a history of  stutterers, nonreaders, or grandmothers whose spelling was charmingly erratic.

Within the past year, Dr. James J. A. Cavanaugh has noted another puzzling incidence of dyslexia in children whose family has a pattern of graying prematurely.

## THE BIRTH PROCESS

Was there any abnormal activity of the fetus *in utero*?

The mother or gynocologist can provide this information.

How did the baby present himself at birth? One obstetrician has formulated the interesting theory that the baby that pushes itself down the birth canal with its right hand will be right-handed; if it strokes ahead with its left, left-handed. The child who strokes himself down using both hands, not only has the beginnings of a good crawl stroke, but has set a pattern of indeterminate dominance that will confuse the signals being sent along to the brain via the central nervous system.

Was the child born prematurely, or by Caesarian section, or was the experience unusually difficult, such as a breech delivery? Such births may delay the proper maturation process.

Some authorities question whether the disorder might not be the result of mixed sex dominants, and for a while the use of hormone treatments was debated. Dr. Malcolm Critchley contests this theory: "The only effect has been that the poor boys have had additional problems added onto their original difficulties."

## THE FIRST TWO YEARS

Dr. William M. Cruikshank, a pioneer in the campaign to

discourage waiting to see whether the child will "catch up," believes that the alert pediatrician can supply a clinically valid clue by observing the way in which the baby sucks his bottle and the amount he drools. The child with tendencies toward dyslexia often displays the jerkiness in his sucking motions that will become characteristic in other ways, as he grows older; one result will be that he will drool more than "normal" babies.

Other signs that should be watched for, are:

Bed rocking and rhythmic head-banging.

Whether the child crawls unilaterally (right hand and leg together, left hand and leg together). According to this theory, Mike's swimming, the trivial incident when he pretended to crawl in the winter under his old green puff did more positive good for his disability than the phonics, delayed until third grade.

Signs of confused dominance.

Inability to distinguish between dissimilar sounds by six months old.

Inability to speak comprehensible words by one year old.

Inability to walk by twenty-two months old.

No sense of direction at twenty-two months old.

Inability to speak logical two-word sentences by two years old. Speaks in unintelligible jargon, speech is cluttered, or stutter develops.    Soft choppy voice becomes more noticeable.

Resists toilet training.

+AGES TWO TO FIVE

The cluttered speech continues.
Hyperactive or tendency to slump.
Inability to complete simple block construction.

141

Inability to defer gratification, the child demands instant reactions from others.

Impulsive.

Inability to follow sequence in picture books, or loss of interest in a story being read to him. The child will not "pretend to read" as his peers do.

Inability to comprehend simple directional instructions such as "push the truck backward." Confusion of first and last, top and bottom, etc.

The child will act out his emotions rather than verbalize.

Very short attention span.

Lack of participation in group activities such as coloring, cutting up paper, etc.

Lack of depth of vision or coordination required to play with a ball.

Inability to master a tricycle by three years old.

FIRST GRADE

The physical and psychosomatic symptoms of the tensions and confusion caused by dyslexia first appear. The gay, happy baby becomes thin and tense. Allergies such as asthma, and tics such as nail-biting and eye-blinking begin. Tantrums persist beyond the age of five. Nightmares are severe and frequent.

Poor pronunciation and cluttered speech become more apparent.

The child cannot remember which sound accompanies which letter.

The child does not learn to read.

The classical symptoms of developmental dyslexia begin to manifest themselves. The persistant reversal of letters, syl-

142

lables, and numbers, in no establishable pattern. The inability to distinguish between stem letters b,d,p.

The child does not master holding a pencil properly. There is a marked similarity in the writing and spelling of all dyslexic children. There is a discrepancy between the hand used for writing and the dominant hand. There is a characteristic jerky movement in writing, and kinetic overshoot and undershoot, i.e., an inability to fit the letters within the lines.

NB: Any or some combination of all these symptoms are found in most children at the beginning of first grade. They will have disappeared in normal children by the end of the year.

## SECOND AND THIRD GRADES

Without help, all the above symptoms persist and worsen as more demands are made on the child.

The writing difficulties will include not only the reversals of letters, but letters, syllables, and words, either omitted or added in no logical sequence. The writing itself will be labored and uneven.

The child is able to think and absorb concepts but is unable to express them in writing or speech.

Secondary symptoms such as headache and nausea after reading will appear.

The child may remain hyperactive or will daydream, yawn, or actually fall asleep in class.

Concepts of direction continue to be uncertain or nonexistant. As Dr. Arthur L. Benton says, "the child has difficulty orienting himself in space, and if he cannot place himself, imagine how much harder it is to operate with symbols such as letters and numbers."

In a series of tests made by Dr. Critchley, a grade school dyslexic noticed subtle differences in a series of pictures (a difficult task for anyone with less than normal intelligence), yet the same child could not draw an arrow pointing in a designated direction. When this child was shown the picture of a street with the sign SOLW painted across it, he saw no mistake.

## FOURTH GRADE THROUGH EARLY TEENS

The lack of directional sense persists.

Neither writing nor reading improve to grade level, although the child's extraordinary memory may enable him to gain passing or acceptable grades.

The child tires easily when writing.

Able to do problems of reasonable or advanced difficulty but makes stupid mistakes in the most elementary processes, or sets down the wrong answer.

Reluctant to read books because it takes too long. The dyslexic begins to understand his own incapacity to picture words.

By seventh grade he will test at least 2.7 years behind in reading even with his above average IQ.

With an IQ of 154 he may reach tenth grade without help, but will test at fifth grade level in reading. If his assignments are read to him, and if he is allowed to respond orally, he will perform at grade level or above.

Able to build complicated models from kits, following the diagrams, although he cannot read the instructions.

If he feels himself pushed or *is* pushed, he will become passive or disruptive in class.

144

With the appearance of adolescence there is a general sense of alienation from home and family. Personality changes become more apparent and more dangerous both to the child and to society. He may retreat completely into a vegetable-like state of total withdrawal, or burst into total rebellion—to compensate for his frustrations—becoming a truant, a dropout, a delinquent, and even a criminal.

If he believes that his child shows signs of language disabilities, the parent is in a much stronger position to approach the school, once he understands the early manifestations of the dyslexic personality. He should ask if the school gives its first graders the tests devised by Beth H. Slingerland. These may only confirm what the parent guesses, but the results of this testing are scientifically accepted proof that even the most closed mind must accept.

If the school does not test until third grade, there are tests a parent can give to satisfy himself, if not the authorities.

If the child is capable of learning a list of words by rote and able to parrot them back to the person testing him, although unable to spell them out of the position in which he learned them, or use them in everyday speech, he may be dyslexic.

Standing behind the child, the parent can recite similar-sounding words with the easily confused *sh* and *ch* sounds to see whether the child can differentiate between them.

If, in reading third grade material, the child substitutes words or appears to be relying upon memory and pictures to help him along, he should be closely watched for further symptoms. The parent can read a passage to the child that should be within his comprehension and see if he really does follow it.

Parents owe it to themselves and their children—dyslexic

*bag    2    bat    spit    [4]*

At seven David had been labeled practically unteachable until he came into the hands of Miss Ethel Johnston at Ethical Culture School. One of his first papers after four weeks of special instruction might still have dismayed an ordinary teacher. Without Miss Johnston's written interpretation the paper is meaningless.

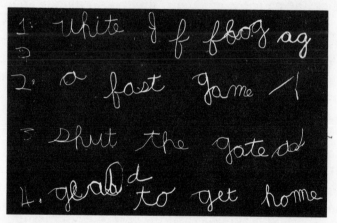

Two months later David is still incapable of writing on a line. He makes a "J" for an "F" but corrects himself. He does not differentiate between the tail of the "g" and the placing of the letter in line with the otherletters of the word. Note that his "M's" have an extra loop, and the letter "d" still eludes him.

Two weeks later he has mastered "m" most of the time, but orienting his letters in relation to space is beyond him. He does better placing the letters of the alphabet.

In February he manages one perfectly legible line.

His last paper in May shows that David, who is of superior intelligence, has worked hard and is on his way to mastery of the written language. In a year he should be working well and with confidence with his peers in his own classroom.                                    147

Ben Our Morning Story Today is Friday. tI is sunny and cold. tI is the last day of the school week We will get our report cards soon.

This mirror writing was a pupil's first attempt at a writing test. When his teacher pointed out that he had written backwards, he turned the page over and wrote correctly However, whether he was writing backwards or forwards he proved to be dyslexic, reversing his *s*,*n* and the word *it*.

Ben Our MorningStory
Today is Friday. tI is
sunny and cold. tI is the
last day of the school
week We will get our
report carbs soon.

or not—to be knowledgeable about the signs and symptoms of dyslexia; the more they know, the more they will demand in help for their children.

There is one drawback to the more general acceptance and recognition dyslexia is meeting today. From being a word so filled with fear and distorted meanings that educators and doctors dreaded using it ("will he have to take drugs all his life?" asked one terrified mother), it is in danger of becoming a fashionable catch-all to include any child with reading and writing problems.

One of the episodes of the popular Dr. Welby series on television during the winter of 1972 centered around a subnormal young woman who had suffered brain damage from a bad fall as a child. When Dr. Welby noticed that she reversed her letters, he diagnosed the disorder as "dyslexia, secondary brain damage," and had his hunch confirmed by a specialist from the Kennedy Center for treating the retarded. "Training her may not make her normal," he says, "but it will allow her to reach her full potential."

It is careless nonsense such as this that naturally frightens the parents of the normal, superbright developmental dyslexic.

There are unscrupulous operators prepared to take advantage of bewildered parents. One eminent ophthalmologist was approached by a franchising firm which offered to set him up with a quick off-the-stove "cure" for dyslexia. Appalled, he answered the letters, drawing out the franchiser by asking what he should do. "In forty weeks you will have your investment back and you will be making money," he was assured.

"What if the children don't learn?" he persisted.

"They come back for a second term," he was told. "Anyway, that's not your responsibility. In education you don't have to prove anything."

At the other end of the scale, perfectly reputable pediatricians and ophthalmologists still know no more about the true meaning of dyslexia and how it can be combated, than Mike's old doctor.

I had reason to visit a young doctor, fresh out of medical school within the past year.

"Tell me, doctor," I asked, "have you ever noted any children with dyslexia?"

"You mean alexia," he told me firmly, and turned to his next folder (obviously these professional men must be nameless).

Recently, an eminent opthalmologist declared, "Dyslexia? Yes, I've treated some cases. Give them eye exercises for a couple of months and it clears right up.

"But most of those boys they bring to me are certainly not dyslexic. I've tried exercises for a whole school term and they still can't read. I don't believe they want to; just too lazy. Of course, you can't tell their parents that."

We shall hear this erroneous opinion echoed several times in the course of the next few chapters.

Possibly the most sensible (and shortest) test for the older child was suggested by a better-informed ophthalmologist:

"If you take the child to the eye doctor and have his eyes tested, and with the help of a few exercises or a pair of glasses he learns to read, he is not dyslexic. If you take him to an ear man and a hearing aid cures him, he did not have dyslexia. If you take him to a psychiatrist and his emotional problems vanish and he learns to read, he does not have developmental dyslexia.

"If none of these help, he does."

150

# CHAPTER

# 13

If we had been content to abide meekly by Collegiate's remedial reading teacher's verdict that Mike was retarded—instead of getting fighting mad—Mike might have finished his schooling in an institution for the retarded, or in jail.

However, our rancor toward this woman does not extend to the school: it had trusted her as its expert.

Yet even in those days, this expert could have learned about Mike's difficulties by walking three blocks east from Collegiate and down to the Ethical Culture School, at Central Park West and Sixty-third Street. There, he would have found an opposite number, trained in the therapies of an American pioneer who had explored the mysterious maze that is dyslexia.

Miss Anna Gillingham taught at Ethical Culture until 1935. In 1919 she had already noted a curious learning pattern in one of her pupils, and wrote about it in the school's *Bulletin*. "Here is a boy who forms only the vaguest visual images; he fails on words studied again and again in the silence of the classroom. He is sent to the rooftop to shout the words into his own ears, with the muscles of his own throat. He remembers them."

Miss Gillingham set herself the task of solving this strange puzzle. While she was pursuing her research in New York, out on the plains of Iowa a neurologist, Dr. Samuel T. Orton—whom I mentioned earlier—was making his observations. In the mid-nineteen-twenties, the state authorized a team made up of Dr. Orton, a psychologist, and a social worker, to evaluate the mental health of children in its public schools.

In January of 1925, Dr. Orton found a sixteen-year-old boy in the seventh grade who could scarcely read or write. He studied this boy intensively, and came to the conclusion that here was a case of "congenital word blindness." Dr. Orton was an excellent organizer as well as scientist. Within a year he had set up a laboratory unit to study language difficulties at the State Hospital, of which he was director. He had also managed to secure a grant of sixty thousand dollars from the Rockefeller Foundation, which allowed him to establish an auxiliary mobile field unit. He was able to examine one thousand and ninety cases. One third had I.Q.'s in the borderline range. Thirty-seven children were the victims of some form of mental disease. But sixteen percent of the children had language difficulties, and Dr. Orton believed it was the tension brought on by their inability to read that *caused* emotional difficulties, rather than the other way around.

In 1928, Dr. Orton came to the New York Neurological Institute, and by the following year, he and Miss Gillingham had found each other. They published the results of their joint research in 1933, and the American study of specific language disability was on its way.

Meanwhile, Mike's friend Dr. Gallagher had been making his own surveys, and in 1948 he published his essay, "Can't Read, Can't Spell" in the *Atlantic Monthly*.

By 1949 there were enough interested professionals who wanted to exchange notes and discuss their findings together, that they associated themselves formally into the Orton Society, named after Dr. Orton who had died in 1948.

Twelve years later, when Dr. Herman Krieger Goldberg, Professor of Ophthalmology at Johns Hopkins, began to wonder about the children with perfect vision whom he was called upon to treat because they could not read, he was able to achieve a forum of international proportions: Reading Disability, Progress and Research Needs in Dyslexia. Psychologists, psychiatrists, ophthalmologists, and hearing specialists attended the conference, but there did not appear to be a plethora of educators. The results of their discussions were published by the Johns Hopkins Press in 1962—just about the time Mike was leaving Harvard for the first time.

Some of the opinions, sagely arrived at, have since been reversed by the same sages. Dr. John Money, associate professor of psychology and pediatrics at Johns Hopkins, was not at all certain that the dyslexic child could ever catch up. College or a professional career was out of the question. Charles Bush, Ph.D., international authority in Oceanic Art on the staff of the American Museum of Natural History, had been told as a boy by no less an expert than Dr. Orton himself that he could not make it through college, since he

153

could never learn a foreign language.

Five years later at the meeting of the National Council on Dyslexia in Philadelphia, Dr. Malcolm Critchley reinforced Money's opinion and added that dyslexics could not hope for important jobs "because they could not do the paper work." It is a pleasure to report that Dr. Critchley appointed himself his own severest critic. He completely reversed himself in a revision of his works in 1970.

The 1961 conference had deplored the disinterest of educators in the problem; in fact, their denial of the existence of the problem. In 1966, Dr. Leon Eisenberg, now head of the department of psychiatry at Harvard, castigated the school system "which waits until the third grade by which time the dyslexic is imprisoned in his faulty learning habits, has become convinced of his own ineptness and now responds poorly to any but the most expert individual clinical instruction." The doctor was discouraged to note that when an enthusiastic convert, a superintendent ot schools in Iowa, asked a teachers' placement bureau for one hundred teachers capable of dealing with children with language disabilities, he was told that there were not more than one hundred in the entire United States.

By 1968 the experts were growing plaintive. They complained that teachers' colleges did not provide even the foundation for special instruction, and little mention is made of specific dyslexia, in special education texts or courses.

Miss Norrie in Denmark, and Dr. Orton and Miss Gillingham in the United States, settled the problem neatly by devising their own systems of teaching. Fundamentally, their philosophies are the same, based upon Miss Norrie's reasonable assertion that "Not the eye but the brain learns to read." In their therapy the brain is given assistance by

154

three senses, sight, hearing, and touch.

Miss Norrie believed in starting with sentences; Dr. Orton and Miss Gillingham with individual letters.

Miss Norrie's system depends on the letter box, of which she spoke in her letter to me. This separates the letters phonetically rather than alphabetically. The letters *m* and *n*, for example, are not even distant cousins, if judged by the mechanics employed to produce their sounds. Yet conventionally they stand side by side, confusing the already confused.

In Miss Norrie's little boxes the letters are assembled according to whether their sounds are produced by the lips, or on the front, or on the back of the tongue. The letters are not only marshaled phonetically; they may be identified by color. Vowels, for example, are red; voiced consonants, green; unvoiced consonants, black.

The teacher begins by teaching sentences using the soft vowel sounds—*big, cat, get, pup*. Each box contains a small mirror, and as the pupil places his letter blocks before him he says them aloud, and watches himself doing so.

The child makes his sentence, and when it finally has no mistakes, copies it out. Miss Norrie and her disciples never pounce on mistakes. Only after the child has announced that the sentence is correct, the teacher may ask, "Do you think some word in the second line might contain an error?"

In this method—and the ones derived from it—the child never works with isolated words. Only sentences that make sense. Completing a sentence correctly may take an hour. The system takes into account the fact that the dyslexic child tires easily. A mistake will be made out of sheer fatigue, the wrong pattern will be registered on the brain, and if the lesson goes on, it will do more harm than good. You will remember that Miss Lever and Mrs. Jackson, whom I found so patient and understanding, kept Mike making the same mistakes over and over, until he became so frustrated that he could not even recall their names when we made the tape together.

Miss Norrie's final admonition was to always end the lesson with praise: "No matter what he has accomplished, he deserves it."

Because of her own personal experience, Miss Norrie did not despair of the older dyslexic. She did have certain rules. They were made aware, in adult, scientific terms, why they had to go back to primer practices; they were never asked to read aloud, not even when they were alone with Miss Norrie. She could still remember how embarrassed she had been by her own stumbling presentation.

She also kept pupils, young and old, at their composition boxes long after they would have been considered proficient in other disciplines. "It is a convenient face-saver; we keep them until the pupil discards them."

I have never seen the original Orton-Gillingham book. The present manual, now in its sixth edition, is called *Remedial Training for Children With Specific Disability in Reading, Spelling and Penmanship*, and Bessie W. Stillman has supplanted Dr. Orton as co-author. It is a weighty volume, both as to size and content. It would not balance comfortably on the stomach for bedtime reading, and it is not intended to. It is written strictly for teachers.

I would gladly have balanced the book—all eight pounds of it—on my stomach if I could have known twenty years ago Miss Gillingham's first rule to teachers: let mothers help their children, let the children dictate answers, dictate whole stories, let them do anything so long as it helps the learning process.

Miss Gillingham understands anxious parents' problems. She cites a typical case history that rang a few bells in our house: The concerned parents take their nonlearner to the most highly recommended reading clinic. "He isn't ready yet," they are told. He is nine or ten. "Give him time."

He is taken to the pediatrician, who weighs him, looks at his tongue, and writes on the card (for his own information) that the child has an overly protective mother.

And if they get as far as the psychiatrist, he asks sly questions about a disruptive home life, sibling rivalries, and whether there is a strong father-image for the child to identify with.

As far as the therapy is concerned, Miss Gillingham suggests that the child go to his regular classes, but have no remedial work there. Conversely, he will do no class work in the remedial class. In this remedial class there will be no—what Miss Gillingham terms—"grunt and groan," phonetics. "Reciting in agonizingly slow harmony "c . . . a . . . t" does not give the right idea of a word."

Gillingham-Stillman teaches children to start with the sounds of individual letters—short vowels first—and build them into words. The syllables may then be cut apart, and the youngster learns that the letters, rearranged in different ways, mean different things.

In this method the children have their boxes, too; they call them their jewel boxes, and they contain syllables as well as short words. As they progress, they make up their own games with them.

Children are made very alphabet-conscious. Younger ones are shown primitive pictographs, Egyptian, Indian and so on. Older ones become interested in Chinese ideograms, and Arabic calligraphy. It is not a course in calligraphy, it is a device for getting attention—and it works.

With a highly trained teacher, the method is simplicity itself. The teacher sounds the letter; the child repeats it. The teacher names the letter or letters; the child writes, naming each letter as he writes. He reads what he has written.

Miss Gillingham recommended that children be taught to read—never mind how or by what method. One of the most prestigious private schools took her at her word and devised a method which is now recognized as a device suited for boys whose vocabularies are more scatological in content than they were twenty years ago.

Tom could not read at fifteen after heaven knows how many thousands of dollars had been spent in the attempt. For one thing, his family would not face the fact that he was dyslexic until he was eleven. Time was running out.

Special tutors had got him through the soft vowels and an assortment of consonants, but the blends—ch, th—remained beyond him.

In desperation, his teacher wrote a word on the board and covered all but the last two letters with his hand.

"It," the boy sounded out.

The teacher uncovered the letter before this. "Hit," the boy said a bit more slowly.

The teacher took his hand away.

"Shit," said the boy automatically, and then waited to be reprimanded.

"Splendid," beamed his teacher, "now we can go on to other four letter words."

The admonitions are as simple: the child *cannot* learn passively, he must participate, employing all his senses. He must not go back to his regular classes too soon. This distrust of

158

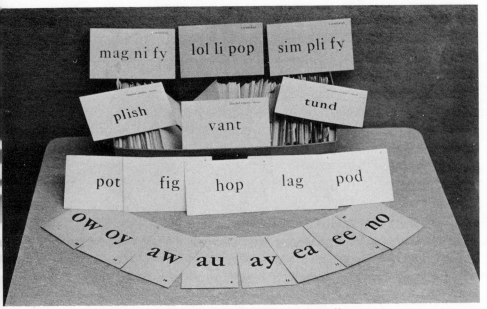

Gillingham-Stillman "Jewel Box"

The Box itself is unimportant; it can be an oblong card catalogue box, or even an old shoe box. The cards—the jewels—come in various groups of colors, each with its own special meaning, filed according to its own category.

In the illustration the second row from the bottom consists of gold cards, the setting that holds the jewels together. These are simple three letter words, all emphasizing the soft vowel sounds, Below the gold row comes the topazes, the deep orange cards that show every possible combination of vowel sounds. These cards are to be read aloud, copied and used to build words in the next step.

Above the gold band are the ruby cards of "nonsense syllables" that are also used to build words as the lessons progress.

The top row contains the sapphires, the real words consisting of a number of syllables, but still divided to show their origins.

159

passivity is crucial. We shall meet it many times in the next few chapters.

The method itself could not only prove disastrous in the hands of the unskilled, but it is not meant for half-hour group sessions two or three times a week . . . "This gives the illusion of helping," Miss Gillingham warns, "and both teachers and parents think the problems should be solved long before it is possible that they can be. The results are a situation twice as bad as the first and much harder on the child, who is now expected to perform at a level at which he is incapable."

Since this last revision, the manual continues to be augmented by the works of Mrs. Sally B. Childs, Miss Gilling-

Ethical Culture also makes use of Sally B. Childs' various workbooks, since these have possibilities for give and take between the teacher and the pupils. No devices are ever used where the child is left with a "workbook" that he must face alone. Participation is everything.

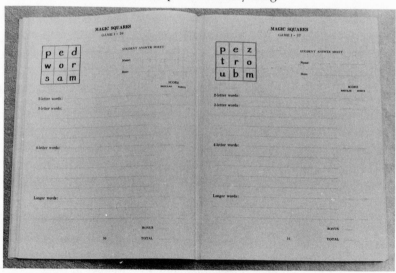

ham's acknowledged literary heir. Mrs. Childs is the author of several books which deal specifically with phonics for the dyslexic child. There is also a gamelike work book, based on the Gillingham manual.

Dr. Archie A. Silver, M.D., Clinical Professor of Psychiatry at the New York University-Bellevue Medical Center, and Rosa A. Hagin, Ph.D., Associate Research Professor of Psychology at the same Center, have devised a teaching approach based on their follow-up studies of children with language disabilities. This approach attempts to isolate and to train out the specific perceptual defects of each child.

Silver and Hagin have been carrying on treatment with a group of children on the lower east side of Manhattan, centered around Bellevue. Their approach is predicated on the belief that once perceptual accuracy, orientation in time and space, is accomplished, the child will then have the basic skills needed to learn to read.

The discipline takes the form of a prescribed series of "tasks" specifically relating to the deficits of each child. Drs. Silver and Hagin point out the training techniques do not offer practice at the intermodal level or the provision for relating perception to written and oral language that they feel is essential to any effective remedial program.

The perceptual stimulation approach requires that each child receive a clinical examination, including evaluation of psychiatric, neurological, psychological and educational functioning, to provide data for a profile of perceptual assets and deficits. This perceptual profile becomes the heart of the teaching program, with instruction focused on the deficit areas which it highlights. The teacher selects from a pool of accuracy-level techniques those tasks appropriate to each child's perceptual deficits.

Training is planned to focus upon the deficit perceptual areas in visual, auditory, tactile, kinesthetic modalities and awareness of body orientation in space. Work is directed toward improving perception through training in three stages: (1) a recognition-recall stage, (2) a copying stage, and (3) a recall stage.

Naturally, among specialists, all these methods are debated as hotly as the "Big Bang" theory of the creation of the universe, or the teachings of Freud, Jung, and Adler.

These are the fundamental systems being used today. Since I was able to visit some of the most successful schools that are dealing with dyslexia, I will show how these systems work and how they are adapted in practice later in the book.

Some of the therapies suggested are less easy to accomplish outside the structured setting of a testing room. All therapists stress that the family verbalize, that reading a bedtime story "must become a nightly activity."

I mentioned Michael's negative reaction to our verbal meal times and to his stories to a number of specialists, concluding, "and none of it did any good whatsoever."

One of them countered, "How do you know it didn't? You don't know what might have happened to Mike if he hadn't had the stories to walk away from."

Among the other less well-known theories is the Delacato Treatment, named for C.H. Delacato, who conceived it. This concentrates on taking the child back to his crawling patterns and repeating the whole learning process in sequence. This method has been used with success in repatterning brain-damaged children. As with treating the child with minimal brain damage, it calls for a great deal of devotion on the part of parents and helpful neighbors, who must lead the child through the exercises for a set period every day. Even the postures and positions of the child during sleep are monitored in this strict regime.

New images are supposedly set, as volunteers push and pull the child through the exercises. Music is not allowed. Delacato held that the new imprints will be made on the part of the brain normally used to record musical sounds, and this portion must be kept blank for these fresh images. The question of whether the dyslexic should be allowed to listen to music was debated during the sixties. It was much too late to be more than of academic interest to us. The portion of the brain that stores the sensations of music had been in use from Mike's earliest years.

Only recently has there been an about face. Music is form and movement in time and space. It is ordered sound. Any progression of tones in horizontal or progressive association is a tune. Rhythm is order. Children who cannot communicate their inner conflicts remain bottled up. Harmony is the balance between tension and relaxation.

Naturally the validity of this treatment is questioned. Doctors Goldberg and Critchley consider the psychological effect harmful. Dr. Ralph D. Rabinowitch asks: "Will he (the child) interpret this as saying 'now you are crawling, now you are expert on the trampoline (or whatever is the next step), you are having your eyes retrained and some wonderful morning you are going to wake up and read through *The New York Times* with no effort at all'?"

On the other hand, not taking the older pupil back far enough academically is as dangerous. A boy in eighth grade who is capable of performing only at first grade level will fail as disastrously at fourth grade level as in eighth grade, with double the harm to his ego, unless he is able to go back to first grade and build from there.

*dyslexia is worldwide*

Dyslexia is worldwide. As late as 1965, the experts thought that only those unfortunates who had to cope with the vagaries of English and the inconsistencies of the Scandinavian languages were afflicted. (They had forgotten Miss Norrie and the French pupils.) It has now been documented that the brains and perceptual mechanics of little Japanese, Russians, Czechs, and Greeks produce precisely the same problems. Children also are dyslexic in Hebrew, Chinese, Arabic, and Gaellic. At international conferences on the problem the flap on the Iron Curtain is sometimes raised for a few tantalizing glimpses. Dr. Zdenek Matejcek of Czechoslovakia is justly highly regarded in scientific circles and has outlined treatment methods in his country. The authorities take dyslexia with great seriousness behind the Iron Curtain. Dr. Matejcek says that Czech is so consistently phonetic in spelling that one would think there would be no difficulties. Nevertheless, they exist, and Czech children are treated on four levels. At the mildest, the remedial work is part of all ordinary classroom curricula. Children with greater difficulties have special classes, and parents are enlisted to carry out therapeutic techniques for ten or fifteen minutes daily.

If it appears that the child might fail, he is put in a special class of not more than twelve children, all dyslexic, to create a "joyful" atmosphere and help him quickly get rid of his feeling of inferiority. Those with the most severe forms go away to special boarding schools, where "all effort is directed to correcting the difficulty and to healing secondary neurotic behavior."

He also shows that Czech parents are no different from their American counterparts. The first reaction of any Czech parent, told about his child's difficulties, is one of deep mistrust. Next, parents think of the effect on the child's (and their) social relations, and what will be thought of *them* if their child is placed in a "special" class. They ask the same questions: "Is he dull?" "Is he retarded?"

Once they have been converted, they react with enthusiasm and resist sending the child back to the regular schools after he has overcome his problem. Furthermore, they can be as unreasonable as the child-oriented family that is the butt of American jokes. What was good for Pietr *must* be good for Anna or Jan, and it is not fair that he or she should not have the same "advantages" . . . no matter how many times the educators assure them that Anna and Jan do not need these particular advantages.

If Mike were a preschooler today, what sort of reception could he expect, what sort of cooperation and help would his parents receive? The remaining chapters will be devoted to actual visits made to a variety of schools to see what is being done for the dyslexic child in the nineteen-seventies. Fittingly, our first visit will be to Collegiate, where Mike's troubles began.

# CHAPTER

# 14

After twenty years, many things remain the same at Collegiate. Classes go on in the same beautifully mellowed yellow-brick building, now rightly designated a City landmark.

However, in keeping with the times, attitudes have changed. So far as this study is concerned, the most important change is the one toward boys with language difficulties. There is no longer the remotest possibility that a Mike would be branded as retarded, and put on the discard heap at Collegiate. He would not even be allowed to become discouraged. The Collegiate boy with specific language disabilities today finds himself a part of as fine a remedial program as a conventional New York school can offer.

All this has happened under the headmastership of Carl Andrews. When Dr. Andrews left two years ago, the school retained many of his innovations and asked Mrs. Andrews to continue as head of the school's remedial reading program. Her special area is the dyslexic. She, too, is a dyslexic, and she establishes the fact—and the ensuing rapport—with her pupils at once.

Collegiate and Mrs. Andrews—and we will use the names interchangeably, since Mrs. Andrews is Collegiate in the field of remedial reading—first of all make certain that the trouble *is* dyslexia.

The next step is a thorough eye examination, which is mandatory whenever children are having any learning difficulties serious enough for the school to recommend tutoring or outside help. "It is pure foolishness to jump into general (subject) tutoring without knowing where the underlying difficulty lies. It wastes the time of the tutor and is a waste of money for the parent and, again, of the time of the child— particularly the child, where the stitch in time is so important to his future well-being," says Mrs. Andrews.

Dyslexia can involve eye problems, even if the eyes obey the brain. So do the feet and the arms and the legs—"but you train for a swimming meet or a running match, don't you?" she asks practically.

Mrs. Andrews attributes much of her success with dyslexics to the fact that "a normal person is incapable of understanding the suffering of the dyslexic child." One who has experienced, and still experiences the same difficulties, can say "of course you aren't able to do such-and-such." Then she will tell the child why, in terms that he is ready and able to comprehend.

It takes time, work, cookies, milk, and sympathy. But there

is always discipline, always control. Freedom to learn what he chooses, at a time that is convenient, or that amuses and fits in with the momentary whims of the pupil, is not for the disabled learner in the Collegiate program.

Mrs. Andrews reinforces the dyslexic's sense of direction at every opportunity. They go up the RIGHT staircase; walk out of the RIGHT door. When it came to saying "write with your right hand," the confusion existing in the English language added its complications. It helps for a boy to wear his watch on his left wrist, or a signet ring on his right hand. He is en-couraged to use any crutch that helps his confused directional sense.

She is most sympathetic toward boys when they complain of "eye strain" because she knows it is not true eye strain at all. The brain itself has tired, which explains why so many dyslexics stumble badly after only fifteen minutes of reading. Mrs. Andrews tires, too. When she is reading and she feels the first sign of what she calls "the fidgets," she takes out her knitting or needlepoint for a little while, and then returns to her book, proof that her eyes themselves had not tired.

She never hurries her pupils. If a sixth grader is struggling to spell "house," it may take him five minutes, but she does not hover, or fuss, or ask if he needs help. Mrs. Andrews picks up her needlepoint and forgets the boy until he decides he wants help and *he* asks *her*.

She has found that reading poetry aloud to the boys is an excellent device to train their ears and hold their attention. Like Mr. Fry at Saint Bernard's, she picks all the wonderful ones out of old-fashioned childhoods: *How They Brought the Good News from Ghent to Aix; You Know We French Stormed Ratisbon; The Revenge; The Charge of the Light Brigade.* She assumes the boy will stop her if he does not

168

catch what the story is about. He may miss a word here and there, of course, but it is the comprehension she is after, and she is not going to spoil that by stopping for a grammar lesson.

A method dear to the heart of the typical remedial teacher is to ask for rhyming words, but as Mrs. Andrews points out, the dyslexic cannot find a rhyming word that makes any sense when he isn't sure of the pronunciation in the first place. When she uses this particular tactic, Mrs. Andrews supplies the rhyming word, so as to add to the vocabulary and reinforce the spelling of the first word: *bat, cat, hat; see, bee; merry, berry; grade, jade, made,* but not *raid, played* or *weighed.*

The boys who come to Mrs. Andrews never play those group games designed to reinforce memory. There is always a chance that the letters will float, the chain of information falter, and anything that builds up the slightest tension in the pupil, even friendly competition, defeats the whole purpose. That is not to say there is no game playing. It goes on at each session between Mrs. Andrews and her pupil. The games she uses, distributed through several outlets, have different names and trademarks but the concepts are fundamentally the same. Games which require the proper matching of color sequences to form a word; vowels are yellow, the preceding blends green, the endings blue, consonants red. One game used by Mrs. Andrews is a color-modified form of Scrabble, where the players can build words by matching colors.

Others, again with various names depending on the manufacturer, use pictures, with, say, six objects printed on a card. All must be identified with names starting with soft vowel sounds, or as the difficulties progress, hard vowels or stem letters and finally the blends. Sources for the material are listed

Examples of the commercially distributed word games Margaret Andrews uses in her remedial reading classes at Collegiate.

in the appendix.

Like most good therapists, Mrs. Andrews has studied all methods and complemented them with what she calls her "notebooks," filled with the details of her own particular failures and successes. Over the years she has built up a series of devices to be used in a certain order. Soft vowel sounds are

170

Left, Short Vowel Drill is used to teach short vowel sounds which are difficult to learn because of the very slight differences between them. The child must match pictures with the vowel sound at the top of the column. The teacher starts with "a" and "o", two sounds that are fairly easily differentiated, then adds the other vowels as the pupil is ready.

Right, Vowel Dominoes reinforces the child's knowledge of short vowel sounds. In the horizontally placed domino both ends are the same in that the picture and letter represent the same vowel sound, all other dominoes are unmatched. The object is to build from the double domino matching a picture to its corresponding vowel sound on another domino.

always mastered before progressing to the hard sound. A minimum of consonants are used and learned before tackling the more difficult combinations of vowel sounds, such as *ai ea ou*. Last come the blends, the *th*, the *ch*, the *sh*, the rocks on which so many dyslexics founder.

In Mrs. Andrews's little list, *ai, ei, ou* and *au* are the hardest sounds to spell, enunciate, and remember in the middle of words; *ch* and *sh* the easiest to confuse. Hardest of all to distinguish and pronounce are endings, such as *added, tried,* and *dipped.* English is very hard in its variations: *laugh, taught.* One list of spell-alikes that sound different begins with *sew, new*; several months later a pupil added *few.*

At Collegiate the very young learn those difficult "stem" letters in equally whimsical play. The left hand is cupped and placed at the base of the right hand which is held in a stiff, vertical line to form a *d. Duh* says Mrs. Andrews in a deep Papa Bear voice. *Duh,* echoes the pupil. Then the right hand is cupped and held at the *top* of the stiffly held line of the left hand to form a *p. Puh* say teacher and boy in squeaky Baby Bear voices. The boy then moves the cupped right hand to the base of the left for a *b* and says *Buh* in a contralto Mama Bear voice. The gruff *Duh,* squeaky *Puh* and contralto *Buh* are repeated over and over.

The remedial group in first grade at Collegiate practices under cover of their desks all the time while trying to read. No expensive equipment is involved and each year a new crop of readers and spellers emerges.

Older boys in Mrs. Andrews' class used the British phonetic spelling book that Mike used at Saint Bernards.

From her past experience, Mrs. Andrews knows that what works with one pupil does not necessarily help the next boy who walks into her room. Yet she did work out a way to tell time that has enabled scores of boys to read the clock's dial. Her chart holds four clock faces: one is all yellow; one, half green, the other half remaining yellow; a third, threequarters yellow, the top fourth blue; and then all quarters, green, red, yellow and blue. It has worked like a charm with boy after boy, except for the one for whom the whole system was devised in the first place. He has his master's degree in anthropology and can give you any carbon 14 dating accurately, but he still cannot—as they say—give you the time of day.

And what if a boy never learns to spell? His record is marked that he is very bright (which he must be for the special recommendation) but that he will never be able to spell. This is for the benefit of any other school he attends. Collegiate does not use the word dyslexic on the boy's record since this might connote to the college difficulties the student has already conquered. The language they do employ says to the initiated "this boy has had many problems, most of them have been overcome but he has not mastered spelling and should not be penalized for this minor disability."

Furthermore, if he has not as yet mastered handwriting— which Mrs. Andrews considers the least of the dyslexic's worries—there will be another entry in his record stating that he must not be penalized for lack of this skill. Mrs. Andrews notes with satisfaction that Harvard now abides by Collegiate's diagnosis, and the student is allowed to take all his examinations on his typewriter in a vacant room.

With enrollment reaching the point where walls seem to bulge, typewriters cannot as yet be the answer at Collegiate. There are no vacant rooms. If the boy's problems remain as severe as Mike's were, Mrs. Andrews does not hesitate to recommend sending him to a boarding school—such as the one Mike attended—where there is more of the necessary privacy.

As the heavy wooden double doors closed behind me, I mused that paradoxically, big, hearty Collegiate had been a more rigid school in Mike's day. Now, twenty years farther into its three-hundred-and-fifty-year history it, too, has learned a lesson. All boys do not fit into the same pattern, even the very best boys.

# CHAPTER

# 15

The physical changes at Saint Bernard's were more obvious to me. Now there are the science laboratories Mike would have loved. I understand they have even put heat in the gym. The curriculum remains wedged in the classical mold of another day.

The headmaster who gave Mike the gift and love of Latin, and who spent so many patient hours guiding his reluctant hand over the paper as he tried to teach him to spell and write plainly, has retired; Mr. Strange and his cat, and Mr. Fry and "The Prisoner of Zenda" are no longer there.

Stepping inside the door to the remedial reading room is like stepping ten years into the past; it has not changed. Mrs.

Leistikow not only remembered Mike, she remembered his interests, his hobbies, his ambitions, and asked about him with an interest which could not have been assumed.

When I told her what I was doing, and the questions I wanted to ask her, it was a different matter.

"Dyslexia?" she said. "I'm not at all certain that I believe in it.

"For one thing, I don't think the ordinary teacher is equipped to spot it. It is my opinion that the diagnosis of dyslexia is being made many more times than it is present."

"But . . . but what about Mike?" I stammered, thoroughly puzzled. Mike himself felt Mrs. Leistikow had done a great deal to keep the finger in the dike until he worked out his salvation. "Remember, Mrs. Leistikow? He couldn't write at all, he couldn't spell, and how you worked with him, and Mr. Westgate worked with him and . . ."

"Mike had a terrible problem in coordination," she said. "The true dyslexic, in my opinion, cannot comprehend. He sees the words, he may read the sentences, but they hold no meaning for him."

If she believed this, how had she managed to achieve a method so excellent, so in accord with the best minds for the instruction of dyslexics that she might have been asked to instruct lesser teachers? She also maintains perfect discipline and supreme confidence in her own opinions. How did she view Mike and the dozens of other boys like him she had helped?

To my amazement, she used almost the same words to describe what goes awry perceptually with her special pupils as Mike used in describing his theory of dyslexia to me. The image of an object gets mixed up on the way to the brain. It is the teacher's job to get the pupil to see the image—or series of images—in the correct order. Then when the correct order is straightened out, the teacher should reinforce the impressions, over and over and over again.

"I do know dyslexics. Some of them are good spellers, but you stop them and they have no idea of the meaning of the word. They cannot use it in a sentence, and if you take the word out of a list and read a sentence to them, they have no idea what you are talking about."

What does Mrs. Leistikow do then?

"I get them interested in the meaning of words," she said. "We drill on words, forgetting about spelling. I read them books that interest them, exciting books, and then get them to tell me the story in their own words. If they have missed the meaning and the point of the story, I tell them in my words, and then we go back to the author's. I had one pupil who had very little comprehension. I got to him through *Great Expectations*. We would go on to some part which he simply had to know about and just couldn't grasp. So we would go through the routine. In a little over a year he was reading at his class's level.

"If Mike had been one of those cases I won't admit to," she said, "he would have been nervous, he would have been depressed and unsure of himself. He would have become discouraged, and Mike was never discouraged. Never. He was such a happy, outgoing boy, such a fine boy. You forget; he was the best all-round boy in his class."

I thanked her and executed a rapid *volte face*. Obviously, if the headmaster had not discussed methods with parents, neither had he discussed the emotional problems of students with their teachers.

I was still not satisfied. The charming perversity of Saint Bernard's is one thing, but this was a complete enigma. It was hard to believe that a school not designed to cope with dyslexics could have done so many things correctly simply by instinct.

Several months later chance led me to the solution. I discovered that before coming to Saint Bernard's, Mr. Westgate had been an associate of Dr. Gallagher's at Andover. At the time, Dr. Gallagher was deep in his research into the problems of specific language disabilities. With Mr. Westgate serving as friend, interested listener—and at times, devil's advocate—he had spent many a New England evening delineating his theories, both as to the causes of the mysterious ailment and the therapies which might correct it.

When Mr. Westgate first asked about Mike with those leading questions, he knew from the direction in which the answers were pointing what the problem might be.

Why did he never confide in us or any of his teachers?

The answer lies in the times; it was 1952. There was a stigma attached to the word dyslexia. As Dr. Gallagher had said in his article in the *Atlantic* four years before, "some (teachers) are uninformed; others seem to feel it is a criticism of their teaching if such lads exist in their classes."

Probably Mr. Westgate also had Dr. Gallagher's comments about parents in mind: "Parents resist any explanation of their offspring's failure which involves even a hesitant use of the word *hereditary* or *neurological* or *brain*." There was no reason for Mr. Westgate to believe that we might react differently.

I was not unduly surprised to find that certain of Dr. Schmidt's opinions echoed those of Mrs. Leistikow.

"I truly believe that dyslexia is a much over-used term," she said. "I hear it used too much to explain everything. Parents would rather blame a nebulous something which they cannot help than face up to problems they themselves have created. Dyslexia, specific language disability—all these terms—are in danger of becoming slogans, no more.

"They call this my tutoring clinic, you know," she reminded me, "but you also know that that is a device to get the children to talk freely. It is a face-saver. They call me their teacher instead of their doctor.

"When Mike came to me he had many, many emotional problems, and many of them were not associated with either dyslexia or school.

"My job—what I was asked to do—was to deal with these emotional problems . . . and I did; off and on for seven years. His father bothered him, he was bothered by his relations with you, sex bothered him. He felt very rejected.

"Dyslexia is just one neurological factor by the time a troubled adolescent comes to me for help," Dr. Schmidt continued. "I suppose that is why I am opposed to these hasty diagnoses these days. I agree, certainly many of the emotional problems are ones which the dyslexia itself has created.

"But they do not exist alone. There is always the overlay, the influence of other tensions, unrelated problems, on those of dyslexia. There is the meshing of the frustrations of dyslexia on top of these other problems. It takes a highly trained person to untangle them, to sort them out.

"As a psychologist, I see it as my responsibility to do away with all of these overlays of psychological disturbances before one can work with the disability—the dyslexia—itself."

We had asked Dr. Schmidt to help Mike keep his emotional balance until he could find the strength to face his problems on his own.

And that she had done, magnificently.

# CHAPTER

# 16

I was particularly eager to see the special program that was incorporated into the regular curriculum of the Ethical Culture School in the early nineteen-thirties. The methods used have become so much a matter of course that neither staff, pupils, nor parents can imagine any other approach to teaching language skills in the first grades.

I also had been hearing a lot about the Earl Kelley School on East Sixtieth Street in Manhattan. It was founded in 1968 and totally dedicated to the open classroom policy we see extolled widely in the professional educational journals and the popular press. Earl Kelley was no more planned to help dyslexics than Collegiate, Saint Bernard's, Ethical Culture, or—

for that matter—Harvard. One of its aspirations, however, is to instruct so well and in such a way that the child with learning difficulties will never know that he was a disabled learner in the first place.

What do the conservative Saint Bernard's, the prestigious Ethical Culture and the avant-garde Earl Kelley have in common that allows them to succeed with the Mikes of this world?

I myself had attended many forums at the Ethical Culture school to consider the future of education. Unfortunately, long after it could have helped Mike. On this particular morning I glanced toward the roof with new eyes. There was the precise spot to which Miss Anna Gillingham had sent that boy back in 1919 "to shout out his vowels."

Boys and girls now shout out their vowels to Miss Ethel Johnston, in her classroom on the fourth floor.

At Ethical Culture, therapy for the child with dyslexia has been considered a part of the standard curriculum since 1930. All the pupils, boys and girls, are given the tests devised by Beth H. Slingerland before they finish first grade. Before this highly sophisticated system was devised, parents had been asked to send family histories.

These questionnaires included data concerning the parents' own learning processes and those of any older children. They are based primarily on the list of symptoms included in Chapter XII. Miss Johnston has become so interested in the manner in which these informal family studies duplicate and reinforce the results of the highly scientific Slingerland tests, that she is tabulating them for future documentary use.

Simultaneously, kindergarten and first grade teachers have been observing their pupils for trouble with reading readiness

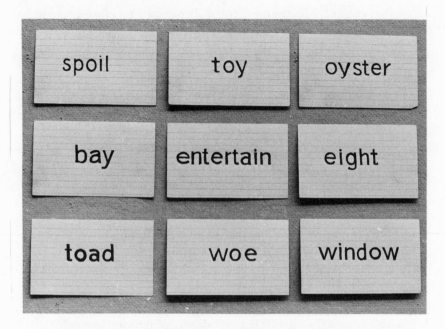

Dissatisfied with a commercially distributed set of cards demonstrating the various vowel combinations that are spelled differently but have the same sounds such as *oi oy,* or *oa, oe, ow,* Miss Johnston had an entire vocabulary of all such sounds hand printed on index-sized cards so that the exercise could be one of group participation, with the teacher always in control. The teacher holds up the cards in succession; the children chorus back the "sound alikes" before writing them down.

The cards may also be collected in the proper sets as a game.

exercises as well as spelling or writing. One of the precepts of Ethical Culture is that the child is not pushed to read before he is ready, often not before second grade.

182

Following Miss Gillingham's edict that all children profit by learning through all their senses, much time during the first two years is given to developing kinetic awareness. The children feel three-dimensional letters by rubbing their fingers over letters made of sandpaper.

Much time is devoted to physical education, where the development of the large motor centers and muscles is stressed.

"Teachers and parents too often overlook that word 'education' when they evaluate gym courses." Says Miss Johnston.

Gym is considered of primary importance at Ethical Culture. It makes for better coordination which must be mastered before one can expect small children to write. The games employ the spatial motion of left to right, and, furthermore, develop the sense of direction so sadly lacking in the child with learning disabilities.

While the children do not actually go back in time and crawl, there are enough childish games where one wriggles through tunnels or creeps across the floor, while the gym teacher watches to see who crawls using opposite limbs and who does not. This will be noted on the observation sheets and will be incorporated in the appraisal of the child's difficulties.

In Miss Johnston's opinion, teachers' colleges do not teach subjects, they teach methods of learning. Once she is in front of a class, the teacher is lost when she discovers she does not teach methods, she teaches *children;* teaches them English, or arithmetic, or history. "There is scant hope for our school system until all our teachers learn the structure of what they are teaching as well as the theories of how to."

With her background, her complete indoctrination in the Gillingham-Stillman teaching methods, and her years of dealing directly with the dyslexic child, no one has more respect for their cleverness, and ability to fox teachers, than Miss Johnston.

Miss Johnston has her own methods for seeing that dyslexic children do not rely on that phenomenal memory of theirs when she is testing them. The child places his pencil on the floor, then the teacher says a word. The child must lean over, pick up the pencil, and position himself back at the desk before writing the word down. This break in his reactions, Miss Johnston maintains, should help in stopping a child from writing a word by rote.

For some reason, many educators and parents cannot grasp the concept that children do not develop all their physical capacities at the same rate; eyesight, aural perception, the kinesthetic skills; all may be on different levels. In children with no disabilities, they all catch up—to the limits of individual I.Q.'s—around the end of the first grade. With the dyslexic child, this is never true, and an important part of the testing is involved with discovering which sense is strongest and which approach to take.

After the testing, the parents of all pupils entering second grade are called in for a group meeting. They are shown a movie, part of a series of three made by Ansara Films for professionals. The first has proven most useful in explaining what the special training will be about, so that parents will understand and cooperate.

The children at Ethical Culture are divided into three groups. The seriously handicapped will have four half-hour periods with Miss Johnston a week. The middle group will have extra work with phonics, but will stay with their class, and the third group are regular students without need of special tutoring. It is impossible not to compare this structuring to the Czechoslovakian system.

Miss Johnston, too, has her rules, as rigid as any that Saint Bernard's or Groton ever devised. First, she insists that everyone—parents and teachers—understand that the child with learning disabilities must have a structured program; *he will fail without it.* (The italics are hers.)

Secondly—more of an aspiration than a rule—she hopes to teach herself out of business.

Her third aim is to have all difficulties straightened out before the end of the third grade. As we have already pointed out, by the third grade the patterns of failure become set, the child is discouraged by failure after failure, and the need for special training or sessions with a psychologist or psychiatrist becomes unavoidable. If a dyslexic child enters Ethical Culture in third grade or later, it is an increasingly difficult job to set him on the right track.

"Motivation gone, certain himself that he is 'dumb,' he is so suspicious of what is being done to him, it may take a whole semester's work to get at him as a person, before the special classes can begin," Miss Johnston notes.

Miss Johnston continued to refer to her pupils as "these boys" despite the fact that Ethical Culture is co-ed. I asked her about it. "The percentages hold," she said. "We test them all, but four out of five children with the disability *are* boys."

Miss Johnston feels that every dyslexic child should be expected to learn to spell, although—as a realist—she knows there are some who never will. She had two prime examples of variants with her when I met her: a boy in the fifth grade who chooses his own outside reading at tenth grade level yet fails third grade spelling, while the other, equally intelligent, is one of those cases that make the dyslexic child an enigma.

He will look at a page and point out every misspelled word. But when the paper is taken away he is literally incapable of spelling a single four-letter word on it. He can't even spell his own name correctly.

Miss Johnston is concentrating on a project to make every teacher in the school capable of spotting the dyslexic child. Since she cannot expect every new teacher to be expert in the Gillingham method, she has put together her own mimeographed adaptation. It simplifies the methods for helping the children in the lower grades.

Miss Johnston is now spending all her free time in the classroom of the second grade, giving pilot demonstrations. She will work on up through the sixth grade—the last, after which the pupils go on to the Society's upper school in suburban Riverdale.

Did Miss Johnston have any hard-core failures?

"One."

He was not a pupil but a parent, and an educator himself. A writer with an international reputation, he was outraged when he was told that his son was to go to Miss Johnston. He refused to permit it. He did not want *his* son to be singled out and "stigmatized." The father diagnosed late maturation. Retested by Miss Johnston, there was not the slightest doubt that the boy was of superior intelligence. He was mature for his age level, but completely dyslexic. Without help, she believes he will not "outgrow" his difficulties.

"We'll do the best we can for him under the circumstances. He's getting phonics with the middle group now, and I can't believe that I won't win over his father . . . eventually."

# CHAPTER

# 17

The staff at the Earl Kelley School is specially trained, totally dedicated and as enthusiastic as the young people who join the Peace Corps.

A short tour through the school reminded me of nothing less than a rock version of Saint Bernard's. Small bodies—whom I guessed to be any age between three and six—were running about, arguing, leaning over tables and squatting under them. The room hummed like a beehive full of busy bees, each intent on doing something of the utmost importance to that particular bee. Pictures were being cut out to illustrate a project; the teacher was seated at a low table reading to a group of children; two small bodies, rather unbelievably wedged halfway under the table were paying rapt attention. Another child had wandered off to a closetlike room, put on headphones and was working with a tape recorder.

Although the teacher was in evidence I thought things could almost go on as planned without her. I was totally wrong, as the principal, Mrs. Eileen McKenna would explain.

The library was the most beat-up room I have ever seen. There were books everywhere, many, many books, very, very used. Again there was a low hum of conversation: "Listen to this!" . . . "You won't believe what it says here" . . . "Hey, Pete, this is really amazing. . . ."

There were two long tables, some chairs scattered in front of the open bookshelves, and four huge, blue vinyl floor-pillows which had seen better days. Boys had taken over the floor, and were twisted on and around the pillows in those tortured postures only boys can achieve. Next to the door, a small girl was curled up on a chair reading *The White Nile*. The place was bursting with energy and kids, not a single one of whom so much as looked up at me standing in the doorway.

The long tables were reserved for children writing and researching papers; they were the source of the scraps of conversation I had been hearing. Sometimes a head was raised in interest at some comment; some did not look up but grunted in agreement; others did not even hear.

There was no teacher in evidence and everyone was studying. I wondered how such disciplined study could occur in this open classroom atmosphere.

"I don't like to call it discipline," Mrs. McKenna replied. "We have an ordered program, an ordered existence, although we are unstructured, but not nearly as much as I'd like to be. We just don't have enough trained teachers.

188

"I am very strong-minded on the subject of teachers who are not trained to handle an unstructured situation and do not have the personality or the self-discipline (she smiled at her own use of the word) themselves to handle an open classroom.

"The present popularity of the open classroom approach will do it a great deal of harm until another new fad comes along to displace it. The unstructured, ungraded, 'open' approach demands a strong, creative, well-trained person to head the classroom. Beyond that, it demands a sense of humor, and a not easily diverted, well-balanced personality. And all the special training doesn't mean a thing if those last attributes aren't there.

"It takes a definite talent to sit on the floor with the kids, and yet manage to stay on top at the same time. In one school I visited, the five- through nine-year-olds were all lumped together. In this classroom the children were good, they weren't running around and they weren't actually killing each other, but by no semblance of the imagination were they learning, either.

"The teacher took off half the class to recite or have special attention; she left those who remained behind with no direction or special suggestions. Some just sat, while some sat and picked their noses, but they were the more active ones.

"The nine-year-olds passed around juice like six-year-olds, and so they acted emotionally like six-year-olds.

"The kids were lackadaisical, bored, argumentative, and talked about everything but school.

"The teacher, as the day neared its end, was plainly on the point of exhaustion. It was her own fault. She had no business saying she could handle a situation-type classroom she was obviously not fitted to handle.

189

"I guess I don't really think of the properly trained teacher as a teacher. The homeroom teacher is really a manager. Everyone teaches some special subject, but there is the team manager to come back to and talk things over with, when the going gets rough. And they have to care as much for the success of their team and the attitude of their team as if they were getting ready to play in the Super Bowl."

I asked Mrs. McKenna why several referral centers had said that Earl Kelley was the best place in New York to send a dyslexic child. She explained that all children are taught at their own level. The goal being that by the end of second grade the disability has been overcome. Each year, two or three confirmed dyslexics will have to be worked with beyond second grade but given the number of children who start out in kindergarten with specific language difficulties, the results are excellent.

Mrs. McKenna devised her own method of teaching reading readiness to "normal" kindergarten children, most of whom did not know what was meant by top, bottom, left, or right. Some of them are going to outgrow this naturally, she pointed out, but statistics say that about a third of them will not. Since it can't hurt any of them, and can save that third, why not try treating them all the same?

At Earl Kelley all the five, six and seven year old children are provided with big, flat sheets, with a sandpaper T at the top and a sandpaper B at the bottom. Down the left side of the page are stars. The children are told to count over from the T to the first star, and write in the white space provided. There are shaded areas between each white space.

Most children will follow the letters across the line with a finger, and in conventional classes they would have a hand slapped for doing so. But at Earl Kelley School the child is

190

given a sandpaper marker to help him get back from right to left, to help train his eye to follow the finger. This is perfect therapy for the dyslexic. Mrs. McKenna agrees with Miss Norrie that dyslexics are so disoriented in space that anything to give them the concept that there is really something special about this left and right bit, is of the greatest importance.

The children dissect the alphabet, breaking down writing into twelve different primary strokes. They then draw the strokes on sandpaper, cut them out, feel them, and make let-

Eileen McKenna evolved the tri-sensory approach to help primary graders at Earl Kelley grasp the concept of letters in relation to space.

The soft flannel background and letters cut out of rough sandpaper overlaid with furry pipe cleaners give tactile reinforcement to the visual effect.

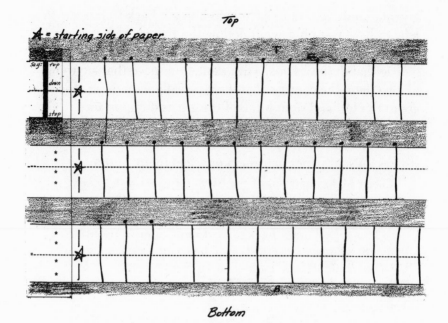

This sheet, with the little sandpaper stick at left is used as an aid in printing at Earl Kelley School. It is also step one in cursive writing. The child moves the stick to the letter space. Without having to keep looking for top and bottom, he can see that printed letters start at the TOP and go down to the bottom of the stick. Cursive strokes start at the bottom and go up to the top. The marker is moved from left to right as the writing moves across the page.

ters out of the sandpaper. Using this method that Mrs. Mc-Kenna developed herself—and others adapted from Gillingham and Norrie—the dyslexic at Earl Kelley can stay with his class, learn with his class, and—except for those few rare cases—remain with it.

The school is named for Earl Kelley, a protégé of Dewey,

who did not misinterpret that genius's teachings. Dewey said "Education is for what is real." He never advocated learning by doing if the "doing" consisted of meaningless, undirected actions, put into a curriculum merely so that the child would appear busy.

Dr. Kelley told a revealing story about Dewey. He stood before his class one day facing the blackboard and proceeded to spend the hour working out a problem in his philosophy, explaining as he went along. The problem was complex. Dewey, given to introspection, was not the world's greatest public speaker, and hearing around his back did not help. At the end of the hour he turned to his frustrated class of graduate students and beamed: "Ah, gentlemen; I believe now that I understand better."

Even this little anecdote has been adapted into a teaching device, that is especially useful in re-enforcing the faltering ego of the dyslexic.

The device involves a "teacher," one of the children; a "learner," another child; and a tape recorder that spews out a lesson. Teacher and learner—whose roles are interchangeable —listen, and then the teacher reinforces the pupil's intake.

It is a splendid face-saver. One day Mrs. McKenna overheard as the "teacher" replayed a tape and then asked for questions, which the pupil answered. "You know," he told his pupil, "I never really understood that myself until now."

What about children who arrive at Earl Kelley only after they have been damaged in other systems?

Mrs. McKenna mentioned a boy who had been brought to her when he was ten; he had been in and out of school after school since he was six. Ridiculed, demoralized, he was literally on the point of destroying himself, even at that early age. Earl Kelley was evidently considered the last resort by his very Establishment family.

In the midst of testing him, Mrs. McKenna asked the boy to describe himself. "I guess you could call me a biological accident," he said, well aware of the line-up of eminent forebears in his distinguished family.

He had an excellent vocabulary, but he could neither read nor write. The school tried all its methods for several months. Nothing worked. Mrs. McKenna felt that the years of frustrations and humiliation had played their part in building up an additional block. The boy refused to even look at a printed page.

One day, in desperate inspiration, she left some source material on dyslexia lying about, and paid no more attention either to the pamphlets or to the boy. Several days went by, and then the boy's curiosity got the better of him. He approached her with one of the sheets and asked what some of the words were.

The upshot was that the mother moved to New York from California to make a home for her boy, and the father flies in to visit with them once a month. Jerry has been at Kelley for two years, and Mrs. McKenna is certain that in one more year he will have caught up with his peers.

There was one revealing incident during his second year. Mrs. McKenna wrote the word "Institution" on the blackboard. The children could elect to treat it whichever way they chose. They could write down one word or they could write an essay. But the next day they would have to back up what they had written and document their definitions and opinions. Jerry wrote down: "Establishment
                    Prison".

At the beginning of the previous chapter I asked why Saint

194

Bernard's, Ethical Culture, and Earl Kelley are consistently successful in training dyslexics. The answer is that each school has its own very different brand of discipline, but it is discipline nonetheless. All agree that when the child gets an image of himself as a 'do-er', the job is half done. All hope to send the child on with a sense of identity and self-respect.

Mrs. McKenna voices the common philosophy, "We do not say 'Come here and be happy;' we say 'come here and be successful.' "

# CHAPTER

# 18

So far, discussion about the methods and the therapies used in the treatment of the dyslexic child has centered around the programs in the independent schools.

In the opinion of most egalitarian-minded educators, the opportunity to attempt this sort of experimentation is a primary justification for the existence of the private or independent school—for independent is what it is: there is less red tape and there are no tax-conscious communities to contend with before a project can get off the ground.

If the experiment succeeds, ideally it will become a pilot for adoption on a larger scale by the public school systems. Unfortunately, the public schools often fail to take the profferred research.

Because of the sheer weight of the problems and the variety of students from different social and ethnic backgrounds, the plight of the dyslexic in the public schools of the nation is bound to have certain fundamental characteristics common to all. One city may have dealt with these problems in slightly different ways from the others. However, this does not change the fact of the universality of the problem.

Most of this chapter focuses on the New York public schools, because they present a viable microcosm to probe, in depth, as we turn to public education. In the appendix, the reader will find a list of other states, and school systems that not only show awareness of the existence of the dyslexic child, but are doing something concrete about solving this nationwide problem.

Twenty years ago we reluctantly decided that New York's public schools could not give Mike a fair chance. The encounters I have had with the system in the past ten years have done little to change this opinion. I remember being taken on a tour of a brand new multimillion-dollar junior high school on East Sixty-fourth Street in Manhattan. There was a theater for amateur plays and entertainments, complete with red carpets, and the latest electronic equipment for the recording and public address systems. There was a vast home economics room, where the latest models of electric stoves and other gadgets stretched into the distance. There were six furnaces for firing ceramics. Finally I came to a large room completely bare of desks, chairs, lamps, bookshelves, and books. "This is our library," I was told.

On the other hand, with all the millions being spent on upgrading education in New York City, and all the talk about open admissions at the city colleges, I felt that the picture must have brightened. Surely I would now find adequate programs at the primary levels for the so-called multiple-problem children who, we are told, cost the city even more millions. The fruits of my search, the comments and opinions voiced in this chapter are almost entirely from those who have worked from within the public system for many years.

It is no secret that many of the teachers caught in the public school system do not give it even D for effort, let alone results. A few write books, such as *Up the Down Staircase.* Some—not as talented nor as strong constitutionally—leave for other fields where they feel they have a chance to use the education to which they have devoted so much time and money. Others stay and fight the system. Most, eventually succumb to the lethargy and the nonacademic word from on high, which controls the destinies of children in the silk-stocking districts as jealously as it does those in central Harlem.

In the fall of 1971, when the public schools were faced with a cut in the school budget, one of the first programs in the New York system to be lopped off was the remedial work being done under the direction of the Bureau of Special Reading Services. With a total enrollment in the city schools of approximately 1,100,000 children, the services could be no more than a token toward tutorial help, but even that was something. Eleven clinics in the five boroughs served 5,000 children each year. In each center was a team of a teacher, a psychiatrist, a psychologist, and a social worker. In short, the services could serve only a small percentage of the total of dyslexic children, to say nothing of those with more and less severe difficulties. It will be recalled that as many as fifteen percent of all children are dyslexic, and some two-thirds of these, incapacitated to a serious degree. In other words, there are an estimated 109,000 children in the New York school system today who will never learn to read without special help.

Mrs. Blanche Lewis, president of the 400,000-member United Parents Association, spoke her piece in January 1972, as she turned over her office to another.

"Our children MUST (capitals hers) be taught to read and to write and to speak, to communicate so that they are understood without grunts, groans, and sign language. Candlemaking, the art of revolution, touch-and-tell, are not substitutes for language, computational skills, or scientific knowledge."

Parent groups, she said, "must expend extraordinary efforts to influence public officials. The myth that politics and schools do not mix must be laid to rest."

Miss Vivian Grano, a teacher at Benjamin Franklin High School in East Harlem, has documented a number of pertinent facts.

"Although reading retardation is a primary cause of failure in the high schools, these schools put children who are as much as five grades behind their peers in reading into regular English courses instead of giving them any remedial help."

However, when high school remedial classes do operate, they are worse than nothing at all. Miss Grano continues: "The classes are set up haphazardly, one could say, reluctantly, staffed not by specialists but by English majors, most of whom detest remedial reading."

In some city schools, as many as eighty percent fail algebra, "because they cannot read well enough to understand the problems they are being asked to solve."

Miss Grano suggested that, instead of giving up before it starts, the Board of Education should make a study of methods used in successful private schools, and copy the best of them. She cites a typical public school primary class.

"As it is now," she points out, "Johnny mumbles an answer

which he hopes nobody will hear. The teacher asks Mary to repeat John's answer, which of course she cannot. Poor John is asked to repeat his answer. By this time no one remembers the question except the teacher. . . . Most of the time is spent in picking up the ball. It becomes very boring for all concerned."


For another perspective on how public schools are coping with the dyslexic child, we turn to Atlanta, Georgia, where the Junior League—which has a national policy of underwriting and staffing pilot projects with volunteers—started the Atlanta school for children with specific language disabilities. The mothers of Atlanta call their dyslexics "S.L.D. children," and possibly that is the term everyone, everywhere else has been searching for. (At one point Mike's father had suggested S.O.S., for strephosymbolia, and that might be considered as an alternate.)

The pilot project was begun in the late sixties by the Junior League for youngsters already in the school system. Pupils were diagnosed and the S.L.D.'s put into a special school set up for them—the Whittaker Center—still free, but underwritten by the League. The children stayed there all day for all their classes, forty pupils at a time; not nearly enough for all who needed help, but a start.

After a year at Whittaker, the children went back to their regular schools, where it had been planned that there always would be a room set aside for them with a teacher trained to help with their special needs. It has not worked out quite that way on a citywide basis. There has been pressure to give more space, money and effort to the truly retarded, and the head of the school system has not been able to push through the complete S.L.D. program.

Since Whittaker was conceived as a pilot for the public school system, the Center itself was moved into a public elementary school building and control turned over to the city in 1970.

Whittaker only takes children from grades one through five, although in practice they are ungraded. Younger children are given preference, and the classes are very small, four or five to a teacher. There is no pressure to learn, but there is the definite emphasis on a disciplined atmosphere. Classes are five days a week, from 8:30 A.M. until 2:30 P.M.

The regular teachers all have their masters' degrees in S.L.D. training, and some are working on their Ph.D.'s. Special teachers come in to teach art, music, and physical education, since considerable emphasis is placed on rhythmic exercises.


In New York, too, the volunteer agencies that have always been ready to help out in the city hospitals, jails, detention homes, and after-school centers, play a hand in helping the dyslexic child overcome his difficulties. These latter, unpaid workers, are struggling to keep a spark of interest alive, to hold their charges in school until—by some miracle—bureaucracy will take the responsibility.

The agency that enlists the most volunteers is the Public Education Association, with 1,350 volunteers. This is no diversion for "radical chic" types who like to make cocktail conversation about what they are doing for humanity. P.E.A. will not accept a volunteer unless she pledges herself to give forty-five minutes twice a week to tutoring a child. She must tutor in whatever neighborhood or locality P.E.A. needs her. Since this may involve an hour's traveling time each way if she is sent to the East Bronx or Central Harlem, the volunteer is expected to consider her commitment seriously before beginning her training.

Mrs. Ethel Price, who directs the program, knows that this is a holding operation as far as correcting a child's language disabilities goes, and the volunteers are aware that they cannot administer adequate professional therapy in the time given to them.

They try to get their pupils to focus on the fun of reading. The volunteers are told to make a special effort to find out what might interest a particular child . . . cars, sports, boxing, movie-making, anything in which a boy or girl evinces the slightest interest, and through which they can capture and hold his attention. Next, they explain to the child that he is going to have to acquire reading skills if he is going to learn more about his particular subject. Since the therapy is conducted on a person-to-person basis, any interest, no matter how trivial it may appear to an adult, will be enough to open the door to *wanting* to read.

P.E.A. volunteers never "tutor" classroom subjects. They are not permitted to do so.

"I think we do some things that are more important than merely stirring up interest in reading," one volunteer told me. "I try to get my children to do something—I don't care what—that makes him look good to himself and gives him some kind of self-respect and confidence."

P.E.A. works from first grade through high school. At Haaren High School, in the old Hell's Kitchen section of New York, "where they send us boys when they won't take them anyplace else," as one cynical teacher put it, the volunteers are men, a group of underwriters from a number of insurance companies.

They have discovered for themselves the same dismaying statistics that Miss Grano found at Benjamin Franklin. Many of the boys cannot read at all.

The men did not make up their teaching manual. They use the "want ad" section of the New York *Daily News*. The words are shorter, and the type larger than in The *New York Times*. "It is almost a text in the words the boys will have to know to make it at all in the world," said one volunteer.

"It's the best way to get them to even try to read before they're listed as high school graduates."

The reader will note that the method used by these men picks up some of the salient precepts for teaching the dyslexic. Many of the words break down phonetically into syllables:

"Au-to Body man: Will pay up to $5 per hour. . . ."; "Clerk: a job in Brook-lyn. . . ."; "Men are need-ed for Guards. . . ."

A man reads an ad to the boys in his charge. The boys repeat what he has said, and then dictate the answers to the ads to their "tutor." He copies down what they have said. Now, teacher and boys read the ad together. Before the end of the lesson, the boys copy out the ads themselves, and their answers.

I have already mentioned the research projects Dr. Archie A. Silver and Dr. Rosa A. Hagin are engaged in on the Lower East Side, and Dr. Jeannette Jansky and Mrs. Katrina de Hirsch pursue on the Upper West Side. Many of the children under study were referred directly from the public schools. It is from work with these children, all from the New York Public School System over the years, that many of the observations have been made which have added much to the knowledge and pattern for the future education of dyslexic children everywhere.

Dr. Jansky tested four hundred kindergarten children from a variety of socioeconomic backgrounds. At the end of the second grade she retested the same children. "Fourteen percent of the white girls and twenty-three percent of the white boys, and forty-three percent of the black girls and sixty-three percent of the black boys from low income groups, had failed to learn to read after being exposed to two years of a variety of educational approaches." The National Advisory Committee on Dyslexia has documented that between twelve percent and twenty-five percent of the children from advantaged backgrounds, black or white, fail.

This is not fodder for the argument that black children have lower I.Q.'s, than white. The Jansky tests demonstrate, once more, that boys have specific language difficulties more often than girls; that the child who is dyslexic in his primary tongue is doubly penalized; and that, in an urban ghetto, the schools may be poorer, with no remedial work and children and families are often more action-oriented than verbally oriented.

For fifteen years The New York Infirmary had its own reading clinic on the Lower East Side. Dr. Ruth Bakwin, director of Pediatrics there, had found a large number of children with specific language disabilities, not only among her private patients but especially in the underprivileged children at Bellevue Hospital, where she served as a staff member.

Twenty-five dollars was allotted to the entire program, for materials. In 1955 Dr. Lauretta Bender joined the Clinic, of which Mrs. Fannie Mendelsohn was director. The children were chosen by the standards already set forth in the chapters on definitions of dyslexia.

When the findings of the Clinic were evaluated, Dr.

Bender estimated that from five to fifteen percent of the children in the general school population had dyslexia in some degree. In the children's ward at Bellevue fifty percent of the boys under twelve years and seventy-five percent of the boys from twelve to sixteen were nonreaders.

This reaffirms the findings of Mrs. de Hirsch and Dr. Jansky that dyslexia does not occur in a vacuum.

It is perfectly understandable that some readers will ask, "but what about Head Start, isn't this doing the job? Why do we need all this fuss and extra expense? The government is spending a mint on Head Start already."

Dr. S. Alan Cohen states that if we take into account the prevalence of specific language disabilities we may understand better why such programs as Head Start have failed to live up fully to earlier expectations.

Whatever the delighted reaction of other children, experts who treat the child with specific language difficulties agree with Dr. Cohen. One teacher, a graduate of the Gillingham-Stillman method in teaching dyslexic children, with a doctorate in education, said:

"Head Start is an inanity; it is dangerous and senseless—unthinking. To mess around with a child's life, to stick in that tiny piece of tissue paper between his third and fifth year is worse than nothing. 'They'—the government, the educators —seem to expect that thin, insoluble tissue to magically correct all that has gone before or will come after."

Another teacher who participated in the program had certain successes because, she said candidly and proudly, "I cheated like mad.

"I had those four-year-olds and I would ask them to bring their little brothers and sisters along; then the next year, the littler ones were there legitimately, and I would ask the ones who had graduated to come and 'pick them up.' For a while I managed to have quite a few children with me for three years. I think that did make a difference in their lives."

Similarly *Sesame Street* and the *Electric Company* come in for a lot of criticism from educators who specialize in remedial reading. While the chancellor of the State University of New York announced that he was surprised and delighted when his five-year-old recited the alphabet and told him he had learned it from *Sesame Street*, and middle-class parents consider it the best babysitter found to date, educators in all fields believe that the program only widens the gap between disadvantaged children—for whom it was created—and the privileged children who are going to learn anyway because of their home environment.

If we look at the programs solely in the context of their effect on the dyslexic child, as a therapist points out they are run through much too fast.

One particular segment of *Sesame Street* concentrated on vowel sounds: *ran, run . . . drum.* The *dr* is one of the more difficult blends, and *m* after a couple of *n*'s was guaranteed to confuse a dyslexic.

The program switched abruptly to long vowel sounds: *be, me, see, cheese. Ch* is an even harder blend to master than *dr.*

No allowance is made for the idiosyncracies between English pronunciation and spelling; the phrase "Bert loves Gert" was shown with emphasis on the *er* sound, so the dyslexic learned to spell: *dert, hert, bern.* Big Bird writes "Kirk loves turnips," and there is no explanation to account for the *ir/ur* spelling.

If *Sesame Street* spells disaster for the middle-class dyslexic, it is even harder for the ghetto child who is dyslexic to be compared disfavorably with his little sister, who stays glued to

206

the tube while he gets the fidgets and wanders off; it reinforces his poor self-image, making him feel he can't be as
good or as bright as she is, or he would *want* to stay there.

As a sore will fester if it is not treated hygienically, as the
child who is deprived of a stable home life will experience
more difficulty in becoming a stable adult, so the dyslexic
child is further disadvantaged by his environment, although
the initial disability is congenital.

Dr. S. Alan Cohen, of Yeshiva University, has noted that
many slum children are physiologically immature—"which
can be caused by not enough of the right kinds of food, or too
much of the wrong kind."

Dr. Cohen continues: "Their cultural deprivation includes
many behaviors we see in dyslexia or specific language difficulties. It appears that disadvantaged children have a higher
incidence of perceptual dysfunction (dyslexia) than test
norms predict."

In one primary school in Harlem, the parents had fought
and won the right to have a voice in choosing the materials
and text books. The book they chose for a first reader is excellent in ethnic identification. The text presents situations
within the comprehension of an urban child. The faces in the
illustrations are black and brown, beautifully drawn; the
scene is a crowded community, familiar to the children.

The words on the first few pages include: "one" . . .
"house" . . . "street" . . . "city" . . . "people."

Unfortunately the book retains the look-say method of
teaching. Probably no other reader with a proper ethnic background was made available.

But by the figures of the Department of Health, Education
and Welfare, one third of that class will not learn through the
look-say methods. No matter what the color of the faces in the

207

picture, the words will be as confusing to this third as the similar one about blue-eyed Dick and Jane. And, caught in this third, will be that fifteen to twenty percent of the children of the highest intelligence, whom their community could expect to lead it in the future.

The children at this well-meaning school are fortunately having their education bolstered by a group of volunteers working out of the East Harlem Protestant Parish.

These volunteers put together and mimeographed a first reader based on the Gillingham concepts. It begins with two short vowels and eight consonants.

It is quite possible, without overtaxing the imagination, to put together sounds and compose sentences based on the ghetto life so familiar to these children.

"A rat bit a cat."

"A fat cat is hip."

"A man hit a can."

"A car hit a kid."

"A kid has a bat."

In this experiment, volunteers find that boys at junior high level, who cannot read, are as excited as the little children in first grade by the material.

The classes also bolster egos.

As the children added to their list of "at" words one of the older boys called "vat." There was much hooting from the class—who had ever heard of a word like that?

The volunteer rapped sharply for attention. "Vat," she explained, "is a proper, perfectly good word." She told them what vats were used for. "For instance, you have to have one to make beer in." The children added "vat" to their list of words.

"It was the first time that boy had been picked out as an academic success," she said later. "He never looked back after that small—you might say—accident. God knows where he'd be now if he hadn't learned to read then."

The *New York Times* recently ran a story about the Black Panthers' breakfast program for small children, during which they chant jingles.

"Kill a pig/Up-on a hill," begins a chant. Could Ethical Culture do better? As the Jesuits say, "The end justifies the means."

". . . if you won't/the Pan-thers will."

The Jesuits have another saying: "Give us the child until he is seven. . . ."


The dilemmas, the hopelessness, the misunderstandings on both sides, which will plague the ghetto boy if his dyslexia is not spotted and remedied, can be as clearly documented when the boy leaves school and looks for work.

At one chain of food stores in New York, preference in hiring is given to minority groups. Obviously, the young people do not start at the top, they are given menial jobs at first, but promotion is possible and encouraged. A young Puerto Rican boy got such a job five years ago. He not only had no English and had stopped school in Puerto Rico at sixth grade, he was also badly crippled. He struggled painfully, both with the heavy packages and the English language, which he was trying to teach himself from reading the labels. He became so successful in his self-education that he was able to stop lifting and hauling and run a check-out counter. Then Jorge disappeared.

A year later he came back for a visit. He would always limp, but it was less noticeable in his good shoes, good conservative business suit, white shirt, and tie.

Jorge had been through the chain's training school and he was to be put in charge of his own store.

Another clerk in the same store had had a far easier childhood than Jorge. José was whole, and strong, he had been brought to this country as a baby, and stayed in school through eleventh grade.

After a few months he was sent to the stockroom to bring out a case of soda. He brought out the case, put it on the check-out counter and was turning away when the manager called out: "Hey, José, I said soda."

José looked puzzled. He examined the carton, shook his head, and looked again. "It says 'soda,' " he insisted.

The manager was irritated. "It does not say 'soda,' it says 'cola'. . . . My God, José, can't you even read that?"

José hung his head, but he took one last not-really-believing look before he went back on the job.

I asked the manager about José.

"Can't figure that one out," he said. "He's got a high school education, and he adds up prices in his head like some sort of machine. But he never reads anything right—can't trust him—you saw him yesterday. It's too bad, but I guess he's just too dumb to get anyplace."

# CHAPTER

# 19

So much for the urban communities. But many Americans live in the heartland, in towns and villages that dot the countryside from the Atlantic to the Pacific. Is there hope or help for the dyslexic child here? Statistics do not change, either with family size or economic backgrounds. Thirty-five children plagued with dyslexia out of a school population of two hundred may not be as dramatic as the hundred of thousands in the cities, but the tragedy is as real, and the thirty-five are equally disadvantaged.

So much depends on the individual teacher in these small communities. I visited one such village just outside the New York City commuter's reach.

Five years ago the school board hired a remedial reading teacher, a graduate of Columbia Teacher's College. Mrs. Baker had not only studied everything in print about dyslexia, she was trained in the Gillingham-Stillman method. After a five-year battle, she believes she has won the teaching staff to her side. Most of them no longer believe (as they once did) that it is a reflection on their abilities when she takes a child off to study with her. For the most part, the parents still distrust her and are leery of her.

The school itself is a large, modern building, yet Mrs. Baker's quarters are quite rightly referred to as the old broom closet. The room is not a full four feet wide, it is approximately ten feet long and the ceiling stretches upward to infinity. There is no window, the only light a fluorescent tube on the ceiling. The ventilation comes from a very noisy fan.

Into this cell the teacher has managed to install three very narrow rows of shelves for books; some colorful wall charts; four desks and chairs for the children—there is no room for a desk for the teacher—and a stand barely large enough to support a portable phonograph.

As the children from other classes pass to and fro in the hall outside, everyone stops, jumps up, and peers through the glass top half of the door. When I was there, the four children sitting at the desks never looked up. The most hideous grimaces went unappreciated.

"You mean someone still believes in dyslexia?" Mrs. Baker asked in happy surprise.

She had been so busy with her children, and her teaching, and so few in her provincial little world did believe in it, that she had become quite discouraged about the larger picture.

Mrs. Baker has experimented with other methods of teaching. She has found that the Gillingham approach remains the

212

most satisfactory, but she has had to adapt it to accommodate the four half-hour sessions she is permitted each week with her students. Individual help is impossible; the children study in groups of four.

First comes diagnosis. At the beginning it was the sole responsibility of Mrs. Baker. Now that she is getting cooperation from other teachers, she has to tell them that all reversals do not necessarily mean dyslexia. As she explained to the first grade teacher, many children learn their first words from the cereal boxes propped up on the breakfast table. Pretty soon, a child guesses that any word that begins with "Whea . . ." and is of approximately the same length as the word at the top of the cereal box is going to spell *Wheaties*, wherever he sees it. He will spell *beat* and *heat* easily. But if he has a logical mind, Mrs. Baker found, he will sound out and spell the synonym for "large", "*graet*."

Mrs. Baker has discovered a new way to spot the dyslexic child. When she tells a group of children to underline words, the child who underlines from right to left instead of from left to right needs to be watched, and four times out of five he needs therapy.

She explains what she is trying to do to her pupils in terms that they, as children, will understand. If they fall from their bikes and break a leg, they will have to learn to walk with crutches for a while before they can walk or ride again; that is what they are doing now with their reading.

With the time given to her (not only are the daily sessions short, but an individual child is not allowed to stay in her classes for more than two years) she hopes to have the child through the soft vowel sounds in a semester. Since she rarely gets the child before third grade—and many times only after that—this is expecting a great deal of both of them. The dou-

ble vowels and the difficult blends—those *sh, ch, gr* and *pl*
sounds—and the double vowels in the middle, are hopefully
mastered in another year, with a semester left for practice.

I watched her working with two boys of eleven. If a visitor
had not known that one was competent at tenth-grade-level
biology and the other worked out ninth grade math problems
for amusement, he could not be blamed if he judged both of
them retarded.

*Gl,* enunciated Mrs. Baker. *Guh,* said one. The other only
gurgled. Patiently they repeated the exercise again and again.

Then, in turn, she had each boy shut his eyes and feel her
throat as she enunciated *gl.* The exercise went on for twenty
minutes before the boys, now feeling the vibrations in their
own throats, achieved the sound.

Next, with a very heavy crayon, pressing down with all
their might, the boys wrote a huge *gl* on large pieces of drawing paper, repeating the sound as they wrote until both assured Mrs. Baker they had the combination.

Mrs. Baker produced a list of words, all beginning with *gl,*
except for one. One boy pounced on the word "give" ten
minutes before the other. The teacher consoled the laggard
by pointing out how much alike an *i* and an *l* look, and this
explanation soothed his pride.

I mentioned the fact that earlier none of the children had
as much as glanced up at the procession of funny faces and
hopping feet before their door.

Mrs. Baker echoed Mrs. McKenna's advice that discipline
is essential in teaching dyslexic children. However, they all
tend to be hyperkinetic; it is better to allow them to bang a
desk or even scream once in a while than to burst through
sheer frustration.

The kindergarten teacher also was a private remedial tutor

before she moved to the village. Again, like Mrs. McKenna, she has proceeded on the assumption that a little tactile instruction won't harm anyone and could stop a lot of troubles before they start.

Her kindergarten children have a favorite "game." Mrs. Donald brings out a big, brightly colored bag filled with large, rough capital letters. In turn each child shuts his eyes tightly, puts his hand deep into the bag, feels around among the letters, and finally picks one. Still without looking at it, the child goes to the blackboard and draws what he thinks has been picked. Now he goes back to see what was taken from the grab bag. At first, everyone makes mistakes. But by the end of the year there will be only three or possibly four. And Mrs. Donald sees that those are packed off to Mrs. Baker without waiting for that third grade testing.

Mrs. Baker added some important advice to those who work with dyslexics: Never let anything or anybody—particularly yourself—get out of control. She admits that she can get excited over a child's progress and, while knowing perfectly well that it is better to hold back than to push, she will occasionally give him a shove forward. Ten times out of ten, the child will regress at once.

As I mentioned earlier, Mrs. Baker's most serious problem is with parents. She cannot break through the prejudices and apathy of the community. She has talked to parents separately; she has spoken before the P.T.A. once, but she was not asked back.

She used the simplest terms in talking to both the individual parents and the group. She emphasized how bright these special children had to be. There was no response, just dead, bored eyes.

She tried to make it more dramatic, demonstrating what

could happen if these intelligent children did not get help and encouragement. She succeeded only in scaring those of the parents who did not become more resentful. At the end of the meeting the audience response was overwhelming.

"He's just a lazy kid; what he needs is a good slapping."

"He always was stupider than his sister."

"He's never going to amount to anything anyway, so what does he need to read all that stuff for?"

"Always was a mean little son of a gun. Just say the word and let me handle things and I'll thrash some sense in him."

Yet among those hostile faces at the P.T.A. were parents whose school records show that they were dyslexics—as were their parents.

Carefully concealing the names, she got out the records of boys from two of these families. We'll call the first Benjy.

Benjy's family came to these shores over two hundred years ago. His relatives are legion and the family has neither deteriorated nor dissipated its holdings in land and more solid earthly goods. They are proud—the "natives" who despise the Madison Avenue types who show up for the summer and fall weekends. They are sensitive, too, and any overt suggestion that language disability could be hereditary is interpreted as a deliberate insult.

At the end of the third grade, Benjy was still writing 25 for 52. Benjy's older cousin dropped out of high school after one year because he could not read, and Benjy has two younger brothers who are displaying the same symptoms. Mrs. Baker did not get Benjy until he was in fourth grade. His third grade teacher was still leery of the "broom closet," but even more intimidated by the power held by Benjy's family in all things relating to the community. She had her ideas about Benjy, but she was not going to voice them. Finally, she got so

216

"mad," as she told Mrs. Baker, that she dragged Benjy down the stairs.

"He can't read, of course," she announced, in front of Benjy, "But he won't need to . . . so long as he gets good enough to read figures and help run the family business."

Mrs. Baker soon found why his regular teacher was glad to get rid of Benjy. All her efforts had been devoted to keeping him quiet enough so she could teach the rest of the class. She had decided he was not stupid and lazy as his family insisted, but emotionally unstable.

Mrs. Baker discovered that Benjy literally could not see or hear words correctly at the same time, although he heard sounds and saw objects correctly. After a year of work, he could not grasp the difference in the sound of *ch* as in "charge" and *sh* as in "sharp"; between *d* and *dr.* "Think" and "thank" sounded exactly alike to him—and the child who does not hear cannot read.

Benjy responded to teaching better than any child Mrs. Baker had ever had. He tried so hard and was so engaging that, egged on by his furious parents, he was put into his regular class too soon.

Now he is back with Mrs. Baker, trying harder than ever. As his second year of instruction ends, Benjy has mastered beginning sounds and some combinations of beginning blends. Possibly the kind of mind which made his forebears hang onto what was theirs, has given Benjy the insight to see himself as a problem to be solved. He himself is working out his own system to learn and remember the hard middle sounds.

After this second year, Benjy will get no more tutoring.

He is getting too little help too late. His family will do nothing further—they pay those enormous school taxes and that is what they. pay them for, isn't it? If he remains determined enough and can persevere he will manage to finish high school. Interestingly, he is no longer a tease or a bully or disruptive in class. Are his parents converted?

"I figured that if we whacked him enough at home he'd grow out of it," said his father.

George's family, on the other hand, has been overly sensitive, if still uncooperative. George's father is a dentist and his mother a college graduate. It was taken for granted that George would do well in school, but he was never pushed. In fact, his father could do much better financially in the city, but came back home so that George could grow up in the public school atmosphere of his father's native town.

Success was so much taken for granted that there were no real records of George's accomplishments or failures until trouble struck in the third grade. Then it was discovered that George, who spoke so beautifully and clearly, could not read or write.

His parents paid for private help and guidance. George was tested and probed and examined for three years; apparently no therapy was included, just batteries of test after test, which impressed his parents but was not of much help to George. The verdict at the beginning of his sixth school year: George was suffering from a malfunction of the eyes complicated with emotional problems. He was sent to an ophthalmologist for eye exercises and to a psychiatrist. Absolutely no progress followed. It speaks well for George's emotional health that he managed to hang on at all.

Finally, in mid-November of his sixth grade year, George was allowed to see Mrs. Baker. Her tests showed what could have been obvious: George was performing not a grade below his level, but at first grade competence. And that is where

218

Mrs. Baker started George. His parents were not pleased.

Nevertheless, they were impressed when, in four months, George was reading and writing at third grade level. On the other hand, it was obvious that this was not going to do a great deal to make him shine in sixth grade work. Mrs. Baker suggested the Hansens buy George his own tape recorder. George takes it with him wherever he goes, to his corrective classes, and to all his regular classes, and records each session in its entirety.

Each night he plays back the tapes, his mother reads his homework assignments to him and he does his homework by recording his answers into another tape. Mrs. Baker convinced George's teachers to run off the tapes in lieu of written work. From being one of the school failures, George is now its near genius-in-residence. In April 1972 he won the county science prize.

The Hansens will no more accept the fact that there is "something wrong" back there in George's heredity than Benjy's parents or the other members of the P.T.A. They do not even like to think that his eyes and ears are confusing their messages to George's brain.

Mrs. Hansen gets around her prejudices by telling herself and her friends that she helps George because of his defective eyesight. It actually corrects to twenty-twenty vision with glasses.

During the winter of 1972 his class was studying the optic nerve, a field in which George has more than a passing interest. Between his mother's reading and his own recordings, George wrote a speech to give to the elementary school assembly. It was so comprehensive and illuminating that the principal asked the twelve-year-old to repeat it for the high school.

Later that same week, the class took its test on the subject. George's grade was zero. He could neither read the questions nor write the answers. The principal, who had come to his job by way of an advanced degree in the sciences, decided to take a hand and make his own experiment. He took George into his office and gave him the test orally. Grade: 100.

George's recorder is now his friend, his first friend in school. His dependence on it is touching. So much so that Mrs. Baker became worried about this attachment. The pediatric psychiatrist to whom I voiced her fears replied that George will probably be the first one to throw "that old thing" in a corner when he no longer needs to rely on it.

These are two of Mrs. Baker's success stories. The tabulation of her failures is as discouraging as in any ghetto school—more so, since the help is there, waiting to be used. But this is no Iron Curtain country where parents are forced to help with therapies after school. In Mrs. Baker's class right now are four boys with superior I.Q.'s whose remedial work was started too late, whose parents disapprove, and who will be dropped from the system as soon as these parents can get them out of it.

At the other end of the scale, one of the most interesting experiments in the education of dyslexics has been made by a group of middle-class parents, living in a small community called Rose Valley, southwest of Philadelphia, Pa.

The Rose Valley School was established in the early nineteen-thirties. Among other things, it has proved that parents are capable of running a school of the highest academic excellence, and that all parents do not develop closed minds along with mortgages and children. The school was and is unstructured. In the late nineteen-thirties, the parents became aware of the work of Dr. Orton and Miss Gillingham. They incorporated into the Rose Valley School's curriculum a complete program for the instruction of children with specific language difficulties.

Mrs. Margaret B. Rawson has kept a careful chart of the progress of the graduates of the school, scientifically comparing—for the first time—the end results of this type of education. The careers of twenty boys with the greatest language difficulties were matched with the accomplishments of twenty boys with no handicaps who had been at the top of their classes. As adults, the dyslexics had done as well academically, and achieved successes in their later lives that paralleled and in some cases surpassed those of the "normal" boys.

It was as a result of these findings, published in a book entitled *Developmental Language Disability; Adult Accomplishments of Dyslexic Boys*, (The Johns Hopkins Press; 1968), that Dr. Critchley reversed his dictum that dyslexics could not hope to compete either in college or in the world.

# CHAPTER

# 20

Speaking before the national convention of the American Association for the Advancement of Science, Dr. Margaret Mead, a scientist and a parent, pointed out that in primitive cultures and, indeed, in America a hundred years ago, there were only three cultural skills upon which man's existence depended. It was necessary that shelter and clothing be provided, and that food be procured and prepared.

This is no longer true in the nineteen-seventies. Man must be able to read to implement the other skills or he will not be able to survive. Boys are no longer apprenticed to learn a trade by watching the master craftsman. Girls no longer are valued as bakers of bread or spinners of wool. Machines have taken over much of the drudgery of manual labor, but in supplanting man, machines have forced man to learn the skills of supervision.

A survey projecting that thirteen percent of the adult population of the United States does not have the reading ability "necessary for survival" was published by Louis Harris Associates in 1970. Percentages in population centers varied, but over eighteen million adults in the United States today cannot deal with such fundamental necessities as applications for Medicaid and Welfare aid, Social Security, drivers' licenses and loans, let alone apply for jobs, or do the necessary paper work to hold them.

Of course, not all these adults come within the definition of developmental dyslexia; some have had no opportunities for education, they have low intelligence or are emotionally unstable. However, the percentage almost duplicates the Department of Health, Education and Welfare's estimate of the number of dyslexics in the population.

Dr. Rosa A. Hagin has remarked that there will be one predictable result of this panic-generated concern: yet another panacea. There will be another federally funded organization with an exciting name: *Project Unique;* or *Operation Alphabet.* It will get much attention from the mass media, and give rise to another rash of false hopes. Many people will profit, but not those for whom it is designed.

This can be avoided if parents inform themselves about the problems and use their considerable power to see to it that the organizations already functioning, and the funds already appropriated, are properly used.

President Johnson made a signal contribution when he set up the first National Advisory Committee on Dyslexia and Related Reading Disorders, under the aegis of the Department of Health, Education and Welfare. When the Committee was established, the then Secretary of H.E.W., Wilbur J. Cohen stated: "The ability to read is becoming increasingly necessary for every person growing up in America today. Yet reading disorders afflict children who have access to good instruction. We need to know more about why these problems occur and what can be done to prevent and treat them." The committee was recruited from the fields of education, neurology, ophthalmology, pediatrics, and psychiatry.

Among them were names familiar to readers of this book: J. Roswell Gallagher, M.D., at that time clinical professor of pediatrics at the Yale School of Medicine; Katrina de Hirsch, and Dr. Arthur L. Benton, Research Professor of Neurology at the University of Iowa.

President Nixon followed up with a grant of twelve million dollars for 1970, and another twenty million dollars a year, through July 1973, to diagnose, prevent, and treat dyslexia, by establishing professional training for teachers and model centers for educating children.

In 1970, moving swiftly by government standards, the committee had made the survey in Maryland which gave Mrs. de Hirsch the statistics to compare reading failures in her disadvantaged groups with supposedly advantaged children. You may remember that between twelve percent and twenty-five percent of the children from Maryland failed in reading in the primary grades.

The project of which this Committee is a part has been given the designation of the "Right to Read Program." Its aim is to stamp out illiteracy in the United States before 1980. "By the end of this decade no one will leave our schools without not only the skill to read, but the desire to read." That is a tall order.

224

The chairman of the Right to Read program, Walter W. Straley, vice president of American Telephone and Telegraph Co., was asked what the program needed most. He answered promptly: "More interested parent groups to exert pressure."

New York State, which has cut back spending for education to bare essentials, nevertheless put out one million, five hundred thousand dollars for a study of how these nonavailable funds should be allotted. The day the report was published, it was assumed it was a plan for action. The following day the commission repudiated any such responsibility; it was —the Fleischman Commission said—a call for *study* of the situation, not implementation.

The National Assessment of Educational Progress is engaged in a federal survey of, "what Americans know and can do." Administered by the Education Commission of the States, an independent association of governors, chief state school officers and legislators, some fifteen million dollars has been spent since 1965 and the study was allotted a further six million dollars for 1972.

A report was published by the Education Commission in February, 1972 on the writing capabilities of eighty-six thousand children, aged nine, thirteen, and seventeen, in twenty-five hundred schools, and of eight thousand young adults in their homes. The term "writing" is confusing; the connotation is rather that of "composition": the test was to show how well the mechanics of grammar, spelling, vocabulary, sentence structure, and punctuation had been mastered.

Nine-year-olds showed "almost no command." In the words of the commission: "By the time most students had reached seventeen years old, they had improved markedly." More than half showed "a sound grasp of the basics of written language"—except for spelling and word choice. "Only fifteen percent showed a serious lack of ability." Young adults of twenty-six to thirty-five showed markedly better ability in the rudiments of written expression than teenagers. No opinion was offered whether the gain in writing ability was because of further schooling or maturation. The commission felt this was adequate support for its continuation.

So much for surveys. On a practical basis, California and Massachusetts have been cited as having outstanding remedial help. Yet Mrs. Sally B. Childs points out that even in these two states barely two percent of the ten to fifteen percent of the children in any average classroom will be properly diagnosed before failures block their progress. There simply are not enough teachers trained to diagnose or treat dyslexia. In Massachusetts, the definition of the disorder varies so greatly that parents must make certain the remedial work is what the dyslexic child needs and that he has not been placed with even mildly retarded children.

In November, 1971, a number of cases were cited by the National Society for Children with Specific Learning Difficulties to show what parents of dyslexic children could do in the courtroom. In Pennsylvania, a judge ruled in favor of parents of a dyslexic child who protested that no provision was made for their child, who was placed in a school for the severely retarded. This case could lead the way to suits by other parents who feel that dyslexics must have as much time and money spent on them as on the retarded.

As I write, there are two such suits pending in Boston, brought against the public schools because dyslexic children with above normal I.Q.'s were placed in special classes for the retarded after incorrect diagnoses.

Also at the legal level, parents of dyslexic children could fight for recognition by Internal Revenue Service. A ruling in

226

1969 has paved the way to deduct expenses for "treating, teaching, tutorial, and other special educational expenses, to alleviate a physical or mental defect or illness."

This wording duplicates that of several state laws, and in a sense expresses the definition of the Department of Health, Education and Welfare, that the term "learning disabilities" includes those whom we have defined as having *specific* learning disabilities. The catch is in the interpretation of the definition; some states are more vague than others as to what this connotes; some include, as does H.E.W., children with "perceptual handicaps, minimal brain dysfunction, dyslexia and developmental aphasia." I.R.S. tends to be harder to convince in the matter of deductions for those mysterious children who are of normal intelligence but who still do not learn. However, progress has been made.

In one test case, the parents of a child of normal intelligence, whose "difficulties were caused by congenital damage" were allowed a medical deduction for the special tutoring.

Richard S. Eustis, M.D. has put it bluntly but fairly. "Special teaching is supplied by public funds for the crippled, the deaf, and the blind. The children of whom I write (dyslexics) are expected to pull themselves up by their bootstraps by 'trying.' If the majesty of the law can keep all children in school, it is the obligation of the school to provide this very considerable proportion of its children with instruction suited to their needs."

Children who do not read can affect their parents' pocketbooks in curiously indirect ways. For example, the amount of money allotted to individual school systems is based on attendance. On any given day, there are two hundred thousand children absent from the schools of New York City, and those

227

same schools lose thirty million dollars each year as a result of the truants. Since the classrooms and teacher are already there, a great many special classes could be paid for, out of that thirty million.

Research has shown that most of the truants are from alienated and deprived minority groups. The reason for the truancy, says an article in The *New York Times* of January 30, 1972 is that "there are tens of thousands of pupils who never learned to read in the primary grades, and by the time they reach the upper grades, school is a bewildering and hateful place."

Taking the truants one step farther and to the national level, eight hundred thousand students dropped out of the high school class of 1971. The delinquency rate was the same for these children before dropping out, so that their final solution was another symptom, not a new one. The dropouts had certain characteristics that distinguished them from pupils who remained in school: "they were four times as likely to have failed a class, their delinquency rate had been much higher and their tests on self-esteem much lower."

Perhaps the most interesting study of the dyslexic as a delinquent was made, not by a doctor or an educator but by William Mulligan, chief probation officer for Sonoma County, California. He also is chairman of the committee on the Neurologically Handicapped Child and the Law.

In the spring of 1968, the special supervision unit of the Sonoma County Probation department screened its total case load of sixty juveniles. The wards supervised by this unit contain the most severely delinquent children, all of whom could be committed for their delinquent acts.

Mr. Mulligan and his staff have been concerned with the correlation between dyslexia and delinquency; they did not believe that all dyslexics would become delinquent, but they wondered about the language disabilities of children already having a brush with the law.

The boys were tested according to the school grade they had attained. At eighth grade level, only one out of seven was performing at his grade level. One read at third grade, one at fifth. One sixteen-year-old boy could read only at third grade level.

In the ninth grade there were two boys out of nine reading at grade level, but one was sixteen, and the other fifteen.

In tenth grade there were boys reading at fourth and fifth grade levels. In the continuation school, the record was poorest, with one boy of seventeen testing at third grade level. The percentages were of twenty percent attaining grade level, and eighty percent below.

Twenty-three of the boys reading below grade level appeared to Mr. Mulligan to come within the definition of developmental dyslexia.

The Probation department of Sonoma County has all the statistics that a therapist might need: I.Q.'s of the boys referred, school reports, and a medical history including the pregnancy record (any illness of the mother; hemorrhaging, premature birth; birth process: difficult labor, anaesthetic, accident, respiratory difficulties); childhood illnesses especially any with dehydration or high temperatures, and family history.

"We felt," writes Mr. Mulligan, "that if some of these children had been discovered and properly treated in the early grades, they would have achieved successes which may have prevented their delinquent involvement.

"If they continue to function at their present level or even slightly above, they will not be productive citizens and in all probability will produce families that will—of necessity—be supported by welfare funds. If they continue in their delinquency patterns many of them will be institutionalized, at considerable expense to the taxpayers."

Mr. Mulligan notes that in nearby Renton, Washington, Mrs. Beth Slingerland has developed treatment for fifteen hundred dyslexic children of average to superior ability out of a school population of 13,950. This is expensive, since the method employs fifty-six special teachers.

On the other hand, "each single boy whom we send to a state correctional institution will cost the taxpayers well over four thousand dollars a year," says Mr. Mulligan. The taxpayer should ask himself what he is going to get for his money when that boy leaves the correctional institution, still bright, still unable to function, still unable to read, write, or hold a job, trained only in antisocial skills, and hating the world he never made.

New Jersey has been asking itself this same question. Its prisons have other walls "more formidable, more restrictive. The walls are the printed word; the confinement, the inability to read; the sentence imposed by a discriminating judge, American education."

Those are strong words; they were spoken by Kenneth Wooden, executive director of the Institute of Advanced Politics, at Princeton.

"Our penal system, like every other state, is reaping the tragic and costly harvest of colossal failure in our national educational system in its entirety."

230

When a man or woman leaves prison, the assurance of a job is of the greatest importance. In 1963 the prisoner could look to a labor market which absorbed seventeen percent of the unskilled; by 1975 there will be unskilled jobs for only five percent.

It has been established through testing that the average inmate, male or female, of New Jersey prisons cannot read at fifth grade level, the national standard for literacy. In one institution, the reading level is grade 2.9, at another it is 4.2, and the best is at grade 4.8 level.

Blacks and Puerto Ricans make up seventy percent of the inmate population; fifty-three percent are under twenty-one years of age. Bordentown Correction Center spends more on candy and tobacco than on any attempt to further the education of these young people.

"Young boys and girls, faces already lined in despair and anger, will continue in increasing numbers to fill our detention centers, crippled in the most basic educational skill—the ability to read," says Mr. Wooden. He continues: "To teach all children to read is no cure-all for our social ills, but it will open a new world of opportunity totally alien to them in the past, a world of hope, with a spirit of human dignity. We owe it to them."

Not all of these young men and women are unable to read because of specific language disabilities. But using the statistics of the national commissions, fifteen percent of the white inmates are dyslexics. Because socioeconomic strains of their environment have aggravated the .condition, as many as forty-three to sixty-three percent of the black and Puerto Rican inmates of the New Jersey prisons did not learn to read because they were victims of dyslexia. By definition they are among the intellectual elite, they could have learned easily in first grade, with proper instruction.

In October 1971 a study, "Inner City Children Can Be Taught," was made by the Council for Basic Education. The tenor of its finding was that the fact that ghetto children read so badly lies not with the children themselves or their background; it is the fault of the schools. The study considered that the "disadvantage of poverty homes can be overcome if the proper conditions are present." [in the schools]

Once again, one solution to this problem is Parent Power.

Informed parents can make their demands, and demonstrate that they are demanding from the strength of knowledge, not from emotion. They can demand that testing and instruction begin by the second half of the first grade. They can remind school boards and town councils of Mrs. Beth Slingerland's statement that "no extra money is needed for specific language disability attention. Screening, plus coordination of instruction is the only expense involved. If a small grant is needed to get started, there are such funds set aside under Title VI by the federal government.

"Parents are the power behind special education programs and they are the ones who get the money for these programs. There is no leadership (in this area) from general education; it does not share in these grants. General education is defaulting by failing to meet the needs of specific language disabilities." Mrs. Slingerland concluded.

It is not difficult to take these preventive measures. We have seen that schools as far apart as a kindergarten in a New England village and the highly specialized Earl Kelley School in New York City give what is fundamentally dyslexic instruction to all small children.

There is always the danger that, after reading this book, some inhabitant of an ivory tower will pontificate that what is

232

needed for the dyslexic child is a typewriter in every school-bag, and until we can afford that on a national scale, why bother at all?

The New York Infirmary started its Reading Clinic with twenty-five dollars worth of material.

There are few communities that could not scratch up the money for:

1) A grab bag of capital letters, such as the teacher herself purchased in the New England village.

2) Sandpaper to cut up into letters.

3) Parents or volunteers who could—if nothing else—give the child the sense of someone caring, who would let him dictate to them, and write down his answers for him.

4) Parents in Massachusetts have put together guidelines for parents and schools. Materials include the above. They also recommend bean bags, old pasteboard containers, sheets of newspapers, and the shadows cast by the children themselves when they go out for recess on a sunny day.

A number of sources for other ideas will be listed in an appendix at the end of the book.

While considering what the untutored child is going to cost in the frustrations of his own failures, parents might think what it is going to cost them—in lost hopes and possibly very expensive stopgaps—when it is too late.

It does not cost that much to have a first grade teacher trained in the more sophisticated techniques. A fourth of what it costs for a new floor for the gym, or lockers around the pool. Parents have to decide which they want more.

Teachers' colleges scattered from Michigan, to Iowa, Pennsylvania and Colorado have begun limiting admissions. There is a glut of teachers on the market, a trend that began in the spring of 1971. In 1972, one third of the one million diplomas

233

granted by the nation's colleges were given to graduates who also received certification as elementary and high-school-level teachers. The National Education Association believes that there will be a surplus of 703,800 teachers by 1977.

Some educators are suggesting that these young people be steered into the undersupplied field of remedial teaching. Informed parents can see that it must go farther than that. Indiscriminate, inadequate remedial work does more harm than good.

If instruction in general methodology were dropped from teachers' colleges' curricula, one intensive semester of study would give a primary teacher the skills to spot the dyslexic child. A few extra courses would give her the skills to teach and present materials in such a way that all children would benefit, and eighty-two percent of the dyslexic children would find the help they must have before they become hardcore rejects.

One year of intensive training will give the young teacher the skills to rescue that remaining eighteen percent. At ten thousand dollars a year, and calculating that instruction is given to twelve pupils for two years, the cost per child is some $1,860 for the entire two years.

We have come a long way from the days when Dr. Orton did not recommend that his pupils attempt a foreign language or attend the kind of college which would demand one. And what of Dr. Critchley, who only in 1970 gave up his sincerely held belief that a dyslexic could never hold a responsible job.

The future holds many exciting possibilities, not the least of which is the exploration into reclaiming the grown dyslexic who has had no help. No one as yet believes this possible, but

Miss Norrie was eighteen when she was given up as retarded.

Schools are accepting typewriters, tapes, anything which will let the dyslexic communicate. Harvard allows typewriters into special examination rooms.

Even College Board examinations can now be taken in a separate room, "with service provided for a reader and/or someone to write down the students' oral answers or dictated composition, or the use of a typewriter."

In the spring of 1972 an admissions officer at Cornell wrote to a high school about one candidate: "I appreciate the fact that you called our attention to his history of dyslexia, which would otherwise have had a negative effect on standardized test data." This officer emphasized that parents of college-bound dyslexics make certain their background is known, so that it may be allowed for.

Much time at the annual meeting of the Orton Society in the fall of 1971 was given to consideration of the adolescent and adult dyslexic. There were studies and seminars ranging from the possibility of teaching the adolescent to spell, to suggestions for special courses at college level. Most practical were talks by heads of businesses about the kinds of training needed to overcome reading inadequacies and enable these young people to take and keep meaningful jobs, at all levels of competence.


A therapist at the Yoder Tutoring School in New York was confronted a few years ago by an agonizingly shy young man of nineteen, who finally confessed that he had never been able to learn to read and write. Tests showed him to be a dyslexic, with a higher than usual I.Q. Out of his modest paycheck, he paid for individual instruction three times a week for two years. He learned to read at possibly third grade level.

He dropped out of sight for several months and then returned to admit to his teacher what his ambition in life had been, and to tell her that he had succeeded in fulfilling it.

Before taking lessons, while waiting in a doctor's office, he had picked up a magazine like everyone else and pretended to read. He had had nightmares during which he dreamed that his subterfuge was exposed to the jeers and taunts of the other patients with their magazines.

Now, the week before, he had had to go to the doctor and had picked up a *Reader's Digest*. He wanted his tutor to know that it was the most exciting thing that had ever happened to him. He had been able to read it; really read it. Maybe not all the words, but if someone had asked him, he could have said nonchalantly: "I'm reading such and such." He had rather hoped somebody would. He was very happy.

As I look back, this vignette stands alone in its gentleness in the midst of the countless cruel and bitterly senseless life stories I have come to know about since I learned the nature of Mike's affliction. So many boys, so many young men were cheated of even this small triumph.

I remember Barry, whose conscientious parents brought him into the City three times a week for two years to a famous Reading Clinic, the same Reading Clinic that in 1972 told me it did not recognize dyslexia, "it's all a matter of overcoming their unwillingness to learn." Barry never did learn to read. He had accident after accident, graduating from bicycles to motorcycles to cars. The last crack-up left him fighting for his life and sanity for nearly a year.

And charming, shy Milton, a brilliant only son who found the effort of reading and writing too much for his strength and his emotions. Milton dropped out of sight as a Harvard sophomore and never came home. He was heard from intermittently, in Haight-Asbury, outside Denver, and finally, it was whispered that he had come to earth in one of those Middle East prisons on a narcotics charge.

There was also Sam, who, the day before he was scheduled to leave for the college he dreaded, walked out into the water and was never seen again.

I will always be haunted by the thought of two potential leaders who have disappeared as surely as Sam and Milton.

One was a twelve-year-old black boy who was to be dumped by the public school system in sixth grade. He had never asked for help and none had been proffered. Long before, in the third grade, he had been judged precisely as Mike had been judged. He could not read, ergo, he was retarded. He had been passed along from disinterested hand to reluctant receiver to await the moment when his problem would be solved by his dismissal from school. The operation was as impersonal as the rejection of a faulty machine from the unending assembly line in an automated factory.

Finally, at twelve, he attracted the attention of a more discerning teacher. She guessed he was severely dyslexic, by now almost hopelessly so. But in spite of all this, including the frustration and hostility and rage which had attended every moment of his academic life, the boy had a nonverbal I.Q. of 115. And he displayed an aptitude for mathematics which approached real genius.

But he had missed his place in the assembly line. He had lost too much time. Higher math, science, he will never know. It is very possible that a latter-day Einstein had been lost, How many others are there like him?

I can close my eyes and see another boy, one of the leaders

in the racially torn school system of New York City. A strikingly handsome boy, it was obvious that he was a born leader. The system had passed him into the tenth grade without teaching him to read or write.

As an experiment, a guidance counselor gave him a pile of pamphlets on the history of revolution. In a few days he was back for more. This boy was brilliant enough to comprehend a subject which interested him. At his age, again, there was no place for him to be tested, helped, and shored up to his brilliant potential. He was too brilliant to accept help although the counselor, too, was black.

He dropped out of school, and out of sight. We do not know where he went, but we do know that it was the lack of a few simple tools that should have been his in the first grade that triggered this totally unnecessary failure, this tragedy.

If he becomes a criminal, if he leads riots and burnings and killings, he will do it with intelligence and courage.

He may very well destroy the country that destroyed him.

His story might have been—so easily could have been—the end of the story of Mike.

# SOURCES OF INFORMATION AND MATERIALS

## NATIONAL SOURCES OF INFORMATION

1. DEPARTMENT OF HEALTH, EDUCATION AND WELFARE
   Results of the Commission on Reading Disorders in the United States, (Other publications upon request. 20 copies, $1)

   *Published as a public service by:*
   Developmental Learning Materials
   3505 North Ashland Avenue
   Chicago, Illinois, 60657

   *Direct from the Department:*
   Catalogue of federally assisted programs for dyslexia and related reading difficulties (includes all types of dyslexia nonspecific and organic).

2. THE ORTON SOCIETY
   *National Headquarters:*
   Suite 204
   8415 Bellona Lane
   Towson, Maryland, 21204

3. THE ASSOCIATION FOR CHILDREN WITH LEARNING DIFFICULTIES
   2200 Brownsville Road
   Pittsburgh, Pa., 15210

   Directory listing information for twenty-eight states where it has chapters, as well as organizations in states not affiliated. $1 per copy. (Note: the association includes in its definition children with minimal brain damage. Parents *must* judge the material with this in mind. Also a source for teaching materials, both for parents and teachers.)

# NATIONAL SOURCES FOR TEACHING MATERIALS

1. DEVELOPMENTAL LEARNING MATERIALS
   (See Department of Health, Education and Welfare)

2. EDUCATORS PUBLISHING SERVICE
   Cambridge, Massachusetts

3. ACADEMIC THERAPY PUBLICATIONS
   1539 Fourth Street
   San Rafael, California, 94901
   (Catalogue available upon request)

4. MASSACHUSETTS ASSOCIATION FOR CHILDREN WITH LEARN-
   ING DISABILITIES
   Box 908
   1296 Worcester Road
   Framingham, Massachusetts 01701

   Many materials listed in back numbers of its
   *Gazette,* and in current numbers. Membership (out-
   of-state accepted) $10 a year. Issue of December
   1971 particularly inclusive.

5. REMEDIAL EDUCATION PRESS
   Kingsbury Center
   2138 Bancroft Place N.W.,
   Washington, D.C. 20008

## APPENDIX II

## SCHOOLS, PUBLIC AND PRIVATE; CLINICIANS; REFER-
## RAL CENTERS AND SOURCES OF INFORMATION LISTED
## AND SUPPLIED BY THE INDIVIDUAL STATES.

### ALABAMA

Alabama considers dyslexia one of the components in the special learning disability complex. The state is making progress in the development of training programs for teachers in this area, and the training program was accelerated at the University of Alabama in the fall of 1972. All public schools are being encouraged to identify children with specific learning disabilities, and programs are being established for dyslexic children as trained personnel becomes available.

### ALASKA

Alaska recognizes specific language disability as a category eligible for special foundation funding. Several school districts now have such programs. The University of Alaska provides training for teachers in this area.

### ARIZONA

Arizona recognizes children with specific learning disabilities, defined by state law as those who manifest "perceptual handicaps, brain injury, minimal brain dysfunction, dyslexia, and developmental aphasia." The definition excludes those whose problems are due to visual, hearing, or motor handicaps, mental retardation, emotional disturbance, or environmental disadvantage.

Referrals may be made by school or counseling personnel, psychologists, social workers, or "other appropriate personnel." An evaluation following referral is required; it may be done by

241

either a psychiatrist, a licensed psychologist, or a physician.

Classrooms to be equal to or better than those used to house regular education. Classes not to exceed ten. All teachers to be certified for the learning disabilities program.

In practice not enough funds were voted to carry out the program in 1971-1972. The Department of Education estimates that not more than five hundred children were served. Bills are pending to ensure more funding for 1972-1973 and for 1973-1974 school years.

PUBLIC EDUCATION:

Child Study Services
Phoenix Elementary #1
125 East Lincoln Street
Phoenix, Arizona 85004

Cartwright District
Justine Spitalny School
3201 N. 46th Drive
Phoenix, Arizona 85031

Coordinator of Special Education
Scottsdale Public School
3811 N. 44th Street
Phoenix, Arizona 85018

Pupil Personnel Services
Washington Elementary #6
8610 N. 19th Avenue
Phoenix, Arizona 95021

PRIVATE EDUCATION:

Dr. Elizabeth Hammer
Devereux Day School
Scottsdale, Arizona, 85251

New Way School
POB 1481
Scottsdale, Arizona 85252

242

OF SPECIAL NOTE:

A federal grant from HEW permitted the establishment of a model teaching demonstration in (1) an urban center (2) a rural area in July 1972, with participation from Arizona State University and the Leadership Training Institute, the latter a division of the University of Arizona's Learning Disability Department. This department is outstanding for its training of teachers in this category. The program at Arizona State is comparatively new.

## ARKANSAS

The State of Arkansas does not make specific program differentiation for dyslexic children. However, it does include developmental dyslexia in its category of children with learning difficulties.

MOST OUTSTANDING PROGRAM:

Child Study Center
University of Arkansas Medical Center
4301 W. Markham
Little Rock, Arkansas

PUBLIC EDUCATION:

These programs work through organized resource rooms. For specific localities contact:

Supervisor of Special Education
Little Rock Public Schools
Little Rock (Mrs. Elsie Butler)

State of Arkansas Department of Education
Special Education (Tom J. Hicks, Coordinator)
State Education Building
Little Rock, Arkansas 72201

Special education includes a field service centered around a mobile van which distributes materials, obtained in cooperation with the University of Texas's Special Education Instruction Center. An information retrieval is part of the service. (Program uses a model 6600 computer to match materials with learning problems.) Special Education also instructs practice teachers from the State College of Arkansas.

## CALIFORNIA

State law dictates that a child diagnosed as having specific language disabilities is placed in a fulltime class of eight to twelve children. Works with specialist from thirty minutes to an hour and a half each day.

Program is entirely separate from the programs for the mentally retarded, physically or emotionally handicapped, deaf, or blind. All dyslexics receive instruction based on Gillingham method. No time-limit set on instruction; continues as long as deemed necessary.

OF SPECIAL NOTE

*Full Orton-Gillingham programs in these districts:*

Claremont Unified School District,
Claremont, California.

Palo Alto Unified School District,
Palo Alto, California.

Stanford Research Center
(Sensory Sciences Center)
Menlo, California

Orton Society
University Medical Center
San Francisco, California 94122

Charles Armstrong School
1187 University Drive
Menlo Park, California 94025

Child Development Center
Children's Hospital
3700 San Francisco, California 94119

Phoebe Hearst Pre-School Learning Center
1315 Ellis Street
San Francisco, California 94115

## COLORADO

STATE AND FEDERALLY FUNDED PROGRAMS
FOR PUBLIC SCHOOLS:

Handicapped Children's Educational Act passed in 1965. Defined by this law as all persons between five and twenty-one who are either emotionally handicapped or perceptually handicapped. Developmental dyslexia is a term not used in Colorado. Children with reading problems are classified as educationally handicapped and specific disabilities are diagnosed under a battery of tests and remedial work undertaken on a resource schedule.

Identifying tests include those most approved by specialists in the field of treating the dyslexic: the Wechler Intelligence Scale, the Bender-Gestalt, the Draw-a-Person test, the Wepman Auditory Discrimination Test.

Referrals may be made by classroom teachers, parents, physicians or outsiders, such as Scout leaders, or Sunday School teachers.

After testing, program permits setting up classes for as few as one or two pupils moving toward maximum enrollment. Maxima depend on severity of disability:

*Seriously involved:*
Separate classroom, enrollment of from five to ten.

*Less seriously:*
Classes of ten to fifteen, or regular classroom; special instruction in groups of not more than five. Teachers must hold an endorsement on education of the educationally handicapped.

*Special project:*
The Rocky Mountain Educational Laboratory
Greeley, Colorado

Federally funded operation under Title II. Large staff draws on knowledge of specialists from entire country. Conducts research and develops innovative practices in classrooms and clinics of eight states—Colorado, Wyoming, Nebraska, Utah, Kansas, Arizona, Montana and Idaho.

Program for children with specific learning disabilities begun in 1967, being completed 1973. There were 7,000 second graders tested in 1968 prototype for project.

Also includes teacher training facilities. Laboratory has available sixteen videotapes which are mailed to teachers in isolated districts, rotated at two-week intervals.

*Pilot project:* three-year program for an American-Mexican community, one-to-one basis, use of typewriters.


## CONNECTICUT

PUBLIC AND PRIVATE RESOURCES:
State law reimburses local school districts for two thirds of the money spent to educate handicapped children who deviate intellectually, socially, or emotionally to the extent that they are unable to progress effectively in a regular school system. The rub lies in the local interpretation of "handicapped." However, communities which have set up programs for children with specific language disabilities have not been challenged.

OF SPECIAL NOTE:
The public school program in Norfolk, New Canaan.
The Clinton Teaching Center trains teachers in the Gillingham approach under the direction of Mrs. Sally B. Childs.


## DISTRICT OF COLUMBIA

PRIVATE EDUCATION:
The Kingsbury Center
2138 Bancroft Place, N.W.,
Washington, D.C. 20008

## FLORIDA

PRIVATE EDUCATION:
Bannatyne Children's Learning Center
P.O. Box 90,
South Miami, Florida 33143

Gables Academy
6501 Sunrise Blvd.
Fort Lauderdale, Florida 33134

## GEORGIA

PUBLIC EDUCATION:
The program in Atlanta has been discussed in the body of the book. Since that information was made available, further information has been received. Summer institutes in geographic locations in the state that had no programs for SLD children were held in 1972. Three institutes have trained fifteen teachers each in ten-week programs. Fifteen hours credit in learning disabilities were a prerequisite for admission to the institutes. In the fall of 1972, a two-day workshop of intensive education was given especially to train directors in the field.

The Education Improvement Project
Board of Public Schools
Atlanta, Georgia

PRIVATE EDUCATION:
The Schenck School
282 Mt. Paren Road N.W.
Atlanta, Georgia

TEACHERS' EDUCATION:
Four colleges are now in their fifth and sixth years of giving training for special work with SLD children. They are:

Emory University
Atlanta, Georgia

Georgia Southern College
Statesboro, Georgia

Georgia State College
Atlanta, Georgia (doctorate level in SLD specialization)

Graduate School for Special Teachers' Training
University of Georgia
Athens, Georgia

## HAWAII

Hawaii recognizes children with specific learning disabilities under the definition of the National Advisory Committee of Handicapped Children as of January 1968. It notes that the definition includes conditions referred to as perceptual handicaps, minimal brain dysfunction, dyslexia, and developmental aphasia. It excludes the categories excluded by definition in this book and also by the definition of HEW: visual, motor, or hearing handicaps, retardation, emotional disturbance, or environmental disadvantage.

INFORMATION:

Children's Health Services
Department of Health
POB 3378
Honolulu, HI 96801

The Office of Instructional Services of the Department of Education has available to the public school system a publication entitled *Program Standards for the Specific Learning Disabilities.* It defines the dyslexic child, gives a list of characteristics by which the child may be identified, and outlines a complete program for teaching as well as prevention. The department stresses the important role which must be played by both parents and counselors. There is a paragraph devoted to the importance of the use of volunteers.

Armed Services Special Education and Training Society
Marine Barracks, Bldg. 286
Pearl Harbor Naval Station, Hawaii 96810

Child Guidance Clinic
Kauikeolani Children's Hospital
226 North Kuakini Street
Honolulu, 96817

Hale Ao
1117 Koko Head Avenue
Honolulu, Hawaii 96816

Hawaii Association for Children with Learning Disabilities
POB 10187
Honolulu, Hawaii 96816
　　(Membership $3 annually. Tax deductible)

Learning Disability Clinic
Department of Health
548 Kapuhulu Avenue
Honolulu, Hawaii 96815

Variety Club School
1702 S. Beretania Street
Honolulu, Hawaii 96814
　　(Preference given to children between the ages of three
　　and eight.)


## ILLINOIS

PUBLIC EDUCATION:
All inquiries may be directed to:

Dr. James Chalfant
Department of Special Education
1005 West Nevada Street
Urbana, Illinois 61801

Dr. Harold McGrady, Chairman
Department of Special Education
Northwestern University
Evanstown, Illinois 60201

PRIVATE EDUCATION:
Institute for Language Disabilities
Evanston, Illinois

## INDIANA

INFORMATION:
Department of Neurology
Indiana University Medical Center
Bloomington, Indiana

Orton Society
c/o Mrs. Charles M. Wells
510 Buckingham Drive
Indianapolis, Indiana 46208

## IOWA

INFORMATION:
Dr. Arthur L. Benton
Department of Psychology and Neurology
University of Iowa
Iowa City, Iowa

## KANSAS

Children identified as dyslexics served under designation of learning disabled children. Form of service at option of local school districts. Children may be served by an itinerant teacher, a resource teacher, or in a self-contained learning disabilities classroom.

OF SPECIAL NOTE:
Local school districts are encouraged to initiate preventive programs in the form of developmental primary rooms, where children with learning disabilities are helped to achieve academic success before a failure pattern is established.

All programs are eligible for special education reimbursement.

Legislation passed in 1972 provides additional funds to those already allotted. In 1971-1972 there were fifty approved learning disability programs. Kansas expects to increase the number during each of the next five years, and in preparation, more trained teachers in the area are being made available each year.

For the year 1972-1973 a Child Service Demonstration Project in the area of learning disability was established under Title VI. Teams of teachers including those for regular classrooms, and learning and language specialists, have been made available through multiple learning centers.

Teachers' training: the University of Kansas offers a sequential program. Other colleges in the state are setting up such programs. Certification in the field requires thirty hours of coursework and is equivalent to a master's degree.


## KENTUCKY

Children classified as dyslexic by criteria of this book and the national societies are lumped with all children classified as neurologically impaired. In specific definition, however, pupils eligible for the special classes are listed as those with normal or above normal intelligence whose meaningful I.Q.'s cannot easily be determined because they do not function at their full potential. School districts are instructed to give preference to children of higher educational potential if limitation of class size is a major consideration.

A medical report by a physician, psychologist—and if requested, a neurologist—is required. Neurologically impaired children who are retarded may not be enrolled in any of the classes at any time.

Class size is 6-8 children per teacher. Teachers must have special certification for work in the field. The school day must not be less than four and a half hours, the remaining one and a half hour of the school day to be spent in preparation if the children are not kept in the classroom for the full six hours.

All programs are set up under the funding of the state legislature and under the direction of the division of special instruction,

Bureau of Instruction, State Department of Education, Frankfort, Kentucky.

## MASSACHUSETTS

### PUBLIC EDUCATION:

This State has one of the most comprehensive programs in the country. There are 240 programs for the perceptually handicapped (includes those with minimal physical damage.) Some schools report that fifty per cent of their pupils are enrolled in the special classes.

Of these, ninety-six have programs designed for dyslexics, twenty-nine other school systems have such programs in the planning stages (June 1972). In seventy-five school systems, children are taken out of their regular classroom for special instruction in small, structured groups. Seventy-two percent use the Gillingham-Stillman method; eighty-seven percent use materials to develop directional sense and perceptual awareness following theories of Doctors Silver and Hagin. Ninety-three percent of the schools make their own materials.

Much use is made of Title I and Title VI money from the federal government, for everything from pilot projects to classes which continue through the summer.

### OF SPECIAL NOTE:

Andover, Belmont, Chelsea, Cohassett, Foxborough, Lincoln, Longmeadow school systems.

### PRIVATE EDUCATION:

The Landmark School, Pride's Crossing. Nonprofit arm of the Learning Disabilities Foundation. The Director, Dr. Charles Drake, studied under Miss Norrie in Denmark. Co-ed. Children who do not meet the criteria for specific language disability will be helped to find a place at a suitable school. Founded in the fall of 1971. Math skills are stressed and every pupil is required to learn to type. Average I.Q., 115. Methods lean to those of Miss Norrie with modern additions: Dr. Drake thinks of the problems of the dyslexic as being one of coding: "the dyslexic child comprehends the task of reading as well as anyone . . . but decoding remains difficult."

Eagle Hill School, Hardwick, Massachusetts.

Curry College at Milton, founded in 1871 with the help of Alexander Melville Bell, father of the inventor of the telephone, and himself a pioneer in phonology, was adapted in 1971 as a college for the older dyslexic. For "students of superior intellect who despair of being admitted to a good four-year accredited college because they have difficulty with reading and writing."

INFORMATION:
   Reading Research Institute
   57 Grove Street
   Wellesley, Massachusetts

   Laboratory of Human Development
   Harvard University
   Cambridge, Massachusetts

   Adolescent Unit, Children's Hospital
   Boston, Massachusetts

   Community for Children with Special Learning Difficulties
   Roxbury, Massachusetts

   Massachusetts Association for Children with Learning
   Difficulties
   Box 908
   Framingham, Massachusetts
      (membership includes parents and personnel of both public and private institutions.)

   Orton Society
   Baker Street Road
   Lincoln, Massachusetts

MICHIGAN

Michigan has a statewide Advisory Committee completing guidelines to be used in the program for the learning disabled. Michigan uses the term in the definition as approved by the Department of Health, Education and Welfare.

To date, education for the learning disabled comes under the general heading of experimental programming. Funding is available under state law. There are forty-nine programs in operation in twenty-five school districts. Oakland and Macomb counties have been leaders.

The advisory committee made up of doctors, psychologists, teachers and parents is evaluating programs used both in Michigan and other states. As a culmination of this work, the committee hopes to develop a model both appropriate to and feasible for the education of the learning disabled of the state. Papers and pamphlets which reflect the experiences of Massachusetts and California have already been made available to all school districts.

Equally available are the reports from the programming in the schools of Oakland County, where eight pilot programs were begun in 1960. The Oakland schools employ colored strips for markers to guide the eyes; teaching through earphones; appeals to all the senses, visual, auditory, and tactile, using any technique which may expedite the procedure.

The state estimates there are 25,716 children who can be called learning disabled and perceptually handicapped, out of a school population of 274,304 pupils labeled as handicapped (*i.e.*, including the mentally, physically, and emotionally impaired). Of those judged to have learning disabilities, 8,134 were awaiting diagnosis and 4,025 had been diagnosed and were awaiting placement.

The evaluation of the experimental programs and the available statistics was to be completed by the end of 1972 and a full program submitted for financing by the state.

INFORMATION:

Orton Society
c/o Sister Anna Cryan
Nazareth College
Kalamazoo, Michigan 49704

254

## NEVADA

The Department of Education is at a very early stage of study for initiating programs for learning disabled students. With funds now available the department has set up an office to study the problems.

INFORMATION:
Mrs. Jane Early
Consultant
Department of Education
Carson City, Nevada 89701

## NEW MEXICO

PUBLIC EDUCATION:

State Funds allocated for children with specific language disability for the first time in 1972. Comprehensive programs were funded by private organizations until this time. New for 1972-1973: a pilot program in the northwest corner of the state where Indian, Mexican-American, and Anglo children with learning disabilities are trained. The project was made possible by a grant from federal funds, by the Department of Health, Education and Welfare.

Definition of the learning disabled parallels criteria used in this book with the addition that in testing the discrepancy between expected and actual academic achievement is observed.

Teachers must hold a certificate endorsed for special education.

Children, severely handicapped, placed in self-contained class, with one teacher to not more than fifteen children with paraprofessional support, as well as professional consultants for evaluation and diagnosis.

For the moderate to mild Educationally Handicapped children: Use of a resource room, (the children remain in regular classroom and come to the room for special instruction). Class size not to exceed eight children, not more than twenty-five to thirty to be served each day. (Legislature may change this num-

257

ber in 1973.) An aide to the teacher is required, and information is to be provided for the parents.

Because of the geography of New Mexico, an itinerant program is included, the teacher to minister to not more than twenty-five to thirty cases, in groupings no larger than eight. Instruction is designed for the individual, must be multisensory, and successful learning experiences emphasized for the support of the child.

*The objective:* a minimum of twenty-five percent to return to the normal classroom in two years. However, four years are allotted for this to be accomplished, after which alternate placement will be effected.

*Diagnostic tests:* see Colorado.

## NEW YORK

### PUBLIC EDUCATION:

New York, in the opinion of its Center of Education in Albany, is hampered by too little funds, and not enough political force exerted by parents and other local voters who might use pressures to get bills to aid the dyslexics out of committee. Bills have been passed. These are empty gestures since the monies to implement them have not been made available.

Political pressure is the key. Out of over 760 school districts, only a scant few over one hundred use the Title I and Title III monies which are available to them from the Federal government. The precise number of such districts is not available, since neither monies nor personnel have been given to compile such a list. Again, until public opinion via the polls forces such action, it will not be taken.

Because of this lack of funds, proper teachers' training is neither being given nor are there enough teachers being hired to afford this type of special training.

There are two divisions in Albany charged with the responsibility for special education: the Division for the Handicapped, which includes those with visual and aural handicaps; and the division for reading education which cannot operate properly in the

258

area of dyslexia for the reasons noted above.

There is a State law #4407 which reimburses parents who cannot find proper education in the public schools for handicapped children, but, contrary to ads placed in various communications media, most dyslexic children fail to meet the diagnostic standards to make them eligible for special education.

Albany speaks of certain localities with especially good facilities, of which it has heard or which it has visited but, out of a possible hundred, points out that this must be considered solely as just that—information gained by such visits; the judgments personal ones.

With such qualifying terms the following communities and clinics which work with public school children are worth special consideration.

OF SPECIAL NOTE:

Shendahowa School System

The Learning Center at the State University at Albany

Westchester County #2 Board of Cooperative Education

Monroe County Learning Disability Center

Coney Island General Hospital

The Public School System of the Hamptons, Long Island

Harrison School System

Shelter Island School System

Long Island Jewish Medical Center, New Hyde Park

Learning Rehabilitation Center, Maimonides Community Mental Health Center, 4802 Tenth Avenue, Brooklyn, New York, 11219

New York University, Medical Center, Language Disorders Unit, New York City

New York Presbyterian Medical Center, Pediatrics Language Disorder Center, New York City

P.S. 158, York Avenue at 78th Street, New York, New York

Pace College Reading Laboratory

41 Park Row

New York, New York 10028

Yeshiva University Reading Clinic
Speech, Language and Hearing Center
East 49th Street and Rutland Road
Brooklyn, New York 11203

## NORTH CAROLINA

INFORMATION:
Orton Reading Center
106 North Hawthorne Road,
Winston-Salem, North Carolina 27104

## NORTH DAKOTA

PUBLIC EDUCATION:
North Dakota has nine programs devoted to the education of children with specific learning disabilities. The programs are not centrally coordinated, and vary considerably. Other programs were slated to be added in the year 1972-1973 and more are considered to be in a transitional stage.

The criteria for determining children with specific learning difficulties are also at the discretion of each local school board. However, it is evident that the definition is much more inclusive than that in other states (Fargo includes socially and emotionally maladjusted children; the consultant at Jamestown is coordinator of the school program at the State Hospital and the program includes those with emotional disturbances).

## OHIO

PUBLIC EDUCATION:
Ohio does not differentiate between children with developmental dyslexia and those with minimal neurological damage. Critera for participation in the program: normal or potentially normal I.Q.; potential for success, (return to regular classroom in three or four years); statement from a physician that the child cannot function in a regular classroom.

However, Ohio issues comprehensive battery of questions to aid doctors, such as cautions that these children are not "late bloomers" but are not performing at potential either.

Parents also must fill out a short fact sheet. Excellent indoctrination for parents included to help them not only become aware of the problem but to alleviate their fears after diagnosis has been made.

Program begun in 1957-1958; grown from two classes serving eight children to two thousand children in two hundred and forty classes in sixty-seven school districts and three thousand more receiving supplementary tutoring.

Much stress on early identification. One failing child discovered in second grade had I.Q. changed from 113 to 140. This pupil—part of sample group all identified in second grade and allowed to stay in program until they can adjust to regular classes—now making A's and B's.

Approximately seventy-two percent of all children who participate in program are successful upon returning to regular classes.

## OKLAHOMA

### PUBLIC EDUCATION:

Public School program is under the over-all direction of the department for the education of exceptional children. These children, categorically broken down into precise groups; the educable mentally handicapped, the blind, deaf, emotionally disturbed, crippled, gifted, and children with learning difficulties. Definition of the child with learning difficulties meets standards of those outlined in this book. All must have normal or potentially normal intelligence. The percentage of children designated as having such difficulties is five percent.

The state considers all dyslexics as victims of "a vicious cycle, unless special facilities are provided to provide equal opportunity without branding the child as different."

Teachers for children with learning disabilities are required to have twenty-one semester hours of credit in professional education appropriate to special education. By law, classes must be of not less than five children and not more than ten.

The classroom, although the number of children is small, must be of sufficient size to provide for equipment and space for

261

developing motor coordination and skills. It must be located in a part of the building with the least traffic and disturbing influences.

## PENNSYLVANIA

No explicit program under the developmental dyslexia category exists. A concerted effort has been made on the behalf of children with brain damage or the psychologically disabled child.

OF SPECIAL NOTE:

Bucks County has had a program for children with learning disabilities for a number of years. A book giving more specific information on one school district may be had by writing to:

Dr. Joseph Tezza
Director of Special Education
Bucks County Intermediate Unit
Administration Building
Doylestown, Pennsylvania
     (Price $5)

*Teachers' Training and Source Material:*
Reading Clinic
Graduate School of Education
University of Pennsylvania

School has established a local Dyslexia Information Center. Also available: a bibliography of over five hundred articles on dyslexia.

## RHODE ISLAND

Dyslexia considered one aspec of total spectrum of learning disabilities. Child so diagnosed comes under programs established for the Educationally Handicapped child.

However, as of May 1972, a task force was set in operation to revise rules and regulations governing education of all handicapped children, and the state expects that specific guidelines will be formulated for children with developmental dyslexia. The state notes that such refinements are relatively new in the concepts of special education.

262

Until the findings of the task force are put into practice, the dyslexic child is recognized as such, but is grouped for remedial work with children with near normal intelligence, perceptual handicaps and minimal brain dysfunction. Confusion may result from this definition. The program excludes those with emotional disturbances, retardation, environmental disadvantages, and defects in hearing or seeing.

Three model projects serve ten of Rhode Island's thirty-nine school districts.

With funds from the Federal Government under Title III centers have been established for the Middletown, Portsmouth, Tivertown and Little Compton areas; for Pawtucket, for East Greenwich, Coventry, Exeter, West Greenwich, Jamestown and North Kingston areas.

There are also six projects with a priority to diagnose children with suspected learning difficulties at Johnston, Warwick, Providence, Coventry, and one to study especially the needs of children in rural districts, working out of Narragansett.

## TEXAS

The language and/or learning disabilities program in the public area in Texas was allocated under Senate Bill 230 in 1969 and has been operational only since 1970. To provide for adequately trained personnel the L/LD program was given developmental status through 1973. During 1970-71, seventeen school districts were selected for the program. Of the seventeen, only five could serve all the L/LD children found in the community. Districts which served a single age group added an additional one for 1971-72. Additional districts were added in the fall of 1972. The program would be offered on a statewide program in all districts for all pupils from three to twenty-one years of age, as of September 1973. The condition termed "developmental dyslexia" is specifically noted and established.

### PUBLIC AND FOUNDATION:

Work with dyslexics in Texas began as a project of the Scottish Rite Hospital in Dallas. By 1964, the hospital was screening

263

children brought in from outlying districts to its evaluation center. As an offshoot, teachers' training programs were set up, so that the children could have proper instruction in home towns. Several courses scheduled for night classes, so that teachers did not have to miss work in their regular class rooms.

OF SPECIAL NOTE:

The hospital itself.

The schools at Lancaster, Texas. Pilot began with eighth grade classes in hopes children would be encouraged to go on to high school. Against all odds and percentages, pupils showed an improvement of forty, fifty, or even sixty points in reading and writing in the Iowa achievement tests. Town doctors now behind this effort, both for funds and aid in diagnosis.

DEPARTMENTS OF SCHOOL SERVICES:

Angelo State University, San Angelo; Baylor University, Waco; East Texas State University, Commerce; Midwestern University, Wichita Falls; Southwest Texas State University, San Marcos; Stephen F. Austin State University, Nacogdoches; Texas Christian University, Fort Worth; Texas Tech University, Lubbock; Texas Woman's University, Denton; Trinity University, San Antonio.

INFORMATION:

Scottish Rite Hospital
Department of Learning Disorders
Dallas, Texas

Mrs. Margaret Booker
Director, Special Educational Instructional Center,
    Material Center
University of Texas
2613 Wichita Street
Austin, Texas 78705

Mrs. Bert Smith
c/o Hogg Foundation
University of Texas,
Austin, Texas

Orton Society
P.O.B. 19112,
Dallas, Texas 75219

## VERMONT

INFORMATION:
Center for Disorder of Communication
Medical Center Hospital of Vermont
Burlington, Vermont 05401

## VIRGINIA

Virginia shows great awareness of the problems of specific learning difficulties and has inaugurated an ambitious program to correct the disabilities.

In its *Standards of Quality for Public Schools in Virginia* (published August 1971) the State Board of Education sets itself the goal that, by 1974 at least 50,000 eligible children will be enrolled in special education programs, as against 37,000 in 1969-1970. This, of course, includes others than those with specific learning disabilities.

In 1964 Virginia gave official recognition to the confusion caused by its existing special education reimbursement programs when it published a pamphlet for educators as a rebuttal to the practice of placing dyslexics in classes designed for the educable mentally retarded. In 1965, with federal funding, classes to train teachers to work with the learning disabled were begun.

In 1969, a committee was convened, to study the problems of the children with learning disabilities, including developmental dyslexia. The committee reported that with all the projected services at the zenith, at least three in every one hundred children would not learn unless individually designed curricula were available. It is also reported "an extreme shortage of trained teachers and a fundamental ignorance of the problem among many already trained professionals." It recommended further steps in reimbursement, better teacher training, the establishment of evaluation

265

centers, and that early efforts be aimed at the early grades, kindergarten through third or fourth grades.

Reimbursement for the disability was made effective for the school year 1970-1971.

At the end of the school year of 1970-1971, a further evaluation was made. The report reiterated that there were not enough specially trained teachers and that parents needed orientation to the problem as well as educators, that supportive services varied greatly from district to district, that since federal funds are awarded for definite projects, more studies were needed, and that principals listed the lack of available space as one drawback to the fulfillment of the plans.

Some results were disappointing: only one school division formally introduced the learning disability program to all division faculty.

New funds were voted by the 1972 session of the General Assembly of the Commonwealth. The Department of Education at Richmond is prepared to be helpful.

INFORMATION:
Ann Sherman, Ed.D.
Assistant Supervisor
Program of the Learning Disabled
State Department of Education
Richmond, Virginia 23216

PRIVATE EDUCATION:
Grafton School
Questover
Berryville, Virginia 22611

SOURCE:
Department of Adolescent Medicine
Medical College of Virginia
Richmond, Virginia

## WASHINGTON

PUBLIC EDUCATION, PRIVATE RESOURCES:
Program for children with specific learning disabilities set

up for school year 1971-1972 under authorization of an Extraordinary Session of the Legislature of the State. Senate bill authorizes excess cost funding to be given local school districts to start and continue such programs.

Service for year 1971-1972 given to 2,691 children. Estimated that 3,425 more were in need of the special education. Total excess cost per child over regular classroom instruction approximately seven hundred dollars. In a self-contained classroom $1,400 per child, which sum includes total educational costs.

Title VI monies from the federal government subsidize twenty-five of the thirty-two Special Study Institutes to train teachers in the methods. Other Title VI funds used to develop three Child Demonstration Centers for children with specific learning disabilities in Seattle, Spokane and Tacoma.

Again, the category includes children with symptoms of dyslexia synonymous with minimal brain dysfunction. State takes cognizance of a difference, but classes as established to date do not.

A self-contained classroom is defined as one in which the pupil received specialized instruction for three or more hours per day.

INFORMATION:
Mrs. Beth Slingerland
Renton, Washington

Orton Society of Washington
143 Fifth Avenue, North
Edmonds, Washington 98020

## WISCONSIN

Wisconsin initiated its first experimental classes for children with specific learning disabilities in its public schools in 1964. (The definition used is that of HEW adopted in 1968 and the one in use throughout most of the states. In practice, the definition approximates that used in this book.) The program was set up at Madison, with Milwaukee following in the second semester of that year. This was considered a major step forward in attempting to differentiate between children who had been labeled minimally brain damaged, neurologically impaired, and the like, for the teacher faced with the problem of handling children with specific learning disabilities with few or conflicting guidelines. Further evaluations and revisions of program are now in process.

Statistically, the Department of Public Instruction estimates the prevalence of specific learning disabilities as equal to the number of emotionally disturbed, almost equal to the number of the mentally retarded (important when the statistics for instruction are noted), and more than the deaf, visually handicapped and other disabled put together, (*i.e.* one-fifth of all pupils with any handicap). Specific learning disability children, in 1969, had twenty-five teachers; the deaf 120; the visually handicapped forty-five; the mentally retarded 1,147. It was estimated that there were 929 teachers for children with specific learning disability with more to be added each year through 1980.

The University of Wisconsin has incorporated a program to instruct teachers in the teaching of children with specific learning disabilities.

### OF SPECIAL NOTE:

The child guidance clinic at Marathon, Wisconsin, under the direction of Dr. Carl L. Kline. In a pilot program, using the Orton-Gillingham-Stillman techniques, success has been achieved with forty-six of the fifty children enrolled for treatment. Added to these traditional methods, Dr. Kline has also experimented successfully with a "catalytic therapy program" for older children who have developed negative attitudes toward the process of learning because of repeated frustration and failure.

## WYOMING

The Department of Education reports that no information is available.

# BIBLIOGRAPHY

Benton, Arthur L. "The Problem of Cerebral Dominance." *The Canadian Psychologist* (October 1965).

Childs, Sally B. "Sound Reading." *Proceedings of the International Reading Association Conference*, 1960.

de Hirsch, Katrina. "Psychological Correlates of the Reading Process." *Proceedings: I.R.A. Conference*, 1962.

de Hirsch, Katrina; Jansky, Jeannette; and Langford, William. *Prediction of Reading Failure*. Harper & Row, 1966.

de Hirsch, Katrina. "The Right to Read—Remphasized." *Bulletin* of the Orton Society, 1971.

Drake, Charles and Schnall, Melvin. *Decoding Problems in Reading: Research and Implications*. City of New York Board of Education, Bureau of Child Guidance. No publication date given. Distributed by Reading Research Institute, Wellesley, Massachusetts.

Eustis, Richard, S. "Specific Reading Disability: Information for Parents and Teachers." *The Independent School Bulletin*, 1948. (Revised in pamphlet form in 1954 for use in the Adolescent Unit of the Children's Medical Center, Boston.)

Gallagher, J. Roswell. "Can't Read, Can't Spell." *The Atlantic Monthly* (June, 1948). Reprints available from the Orton Society.

Gallagher, J. Roswell. *Understanding Your Son's Adolescence*. Little, Brown, Little, 1951.

Gallagher, J. Roswell. "Specific Language Disability (Dyslexia)." *Clinical Proceedings of the Children's Hospital* (Joseph Wall Memorial Lecture. 1960).

Gillingham, Anna. "Pedagological Implications of the Specific Language Disability." *Independent School Bulletin* (January 1952).

Gillingham, Anna and Stillman, Bessie. *Remedial Training for Children with Specific Disability in Reading, Spelling and Penmanship.* Educators Publishing Service. 6th (1960) ed.

Hagin, Rosa A. "Practical Applications of Diagnostic Studies of Children with Specific Reading Disability." *Bulletins* of the Orton Society. (1961, 1963).

Hagin, Rosa A. "Perspectives of Specific Language Disability: the Future." *Bulletin* of the Orton Society, 1971.

Keeney, Arthur H. and Keeney, Virginia T. *Dyslexia: Diagnosis and Treatment of Reading Disorders.* Report on the National Conference on Dyslexia, 1966. The C. V. Mosby Co., 1968.

Matejcek, Zdenek. "Dyslexia, an International Problem." *Bulletin* of the Orton Society, 1968.

Mendelsohn, Fannie, and Courin, Pauline. *The Treatment of Reading Disabilities: An Experience of 15 Years at the New York Infirmary Reading Clinic.* Privately printed, 1964.

Money, John, editor. *Reading Disability: Progress and Research Needs in Dyslexia.* Report on an international symposium of experts at Johns Hopkins University. Johns Hopkins Press, 1962.

Money, John, editor, and Schiffman, Gilbert, advisor in education. *The Disabled Reader: The Education of the Dyslexic Child.* Johns Hopkins Press, 1966.

Mulligan, William. *A Study of Dyslexia and Delinquency.* Academic Therapy, 1970. Reprinted and distributed by the California Association for Neurologically Handicapped Children.

Norrie, Edith. "Word Blindness in Denmark: Its Neurological and Educational Aspects." *The Independent School Bulletin* (April 1960).

Rawson, Margaret B. *Developmental Language Disability: Adult Accomplishments of Dyslexic Boys*. The Johns Hopkins Press, 1968.

Rawson, Margaret B. "Perspectives of Specific Language Disability: the Past—What Have We learned?" *Bulletin* of the Orton Society, 1971.

Silver, Archie A. "Diagnostic Considerations in Children with Reading Disability." *Bulletin* of the Orton Society, 1961.

Silver, Archie A., and Hagin, Rosa A. "Specific Reading Disability: Follow Up Studies." *American Journal of Orthopsychiatry* (January 1, 1964).

Silver, Archie A., and Hagin, Rosa A. "Maturation of Perceptual Functions of Children with Specific Reading Disability." *The Reading Teacher* (January 1966).

Thompson, Lloyd D. "Language Disabilities in Men of Eminence." Paper read at the Seventh International Conference on Mental Health, London, 1968. Published by the Orton Society, 1969.

# INDEX

276

277